A PRAYER BOOK
for
THE ARMED FORCES

THE LORD'S PRAYER

Our Father, who art in heaven,
  hallowed be thy Name,
  thy kingdom come,
  thy will be done,
    on earth as it is in heaven.
Give us this day our daily bread.
And forgive us our trespasses,
  as we forgive those
    who trespass against us.
And lead us not into temptation,
  but deliver us from evil.
For thine is the kingdom,
  and the power, and the glory,
  for ever and ever. Amen.

Our Father in heaven,
  hallowed be your Name,
  your kingdom come,
  your will be done,
    on earth as in heaven.
Give us today our daily bread.
Forgive us our sins
  as we forgive those
    who sin against us.
Save us from the time of trial,
  and deliver us from evil.
For the kingdom, the power,
  and the glory are yours,
  now and for ever. Amen.

THE APOSTLES' CREED

I believe in God, the Father almighty,
  creator of heaven and earth.
I believe in Jesus Christ, his only Son, our Lord.
  He was conceived by the power of the Holy Spirit
    and born of the Virgin Mary.
  He suffered under Pontius Pilate,
    was crucified, died, and was buried.
  He descended to the dead.
  On the third day he rose again.
  He ascended into heaven,
    and is seated at the right hand of the Father.
  He will come again to judge the living and the dead.
I believe in the Holy Spirit,
  the holy catholic Church,
  the communion of saints,
  the forgiveness of sins,
  the resurrection of the body,
  and the life everlasting. Amen.

A PRAYER BOOK
for
THE ARMED FORCES

1988

Published for the Bishop for the Armed Forces
The Episcopal Church

CONTENTS

PREFACE

This book is presented to you with the prayer that it will support your faith and also be a valuable tool both in the hours of despair and in the moments of joy.

Like its predecessors, this Prayer Book for the Armed Forces reflects the worship and practice of The Episcopal Church. Most of its contents are taken from the Book of Common Prayer. It also contains information and suggestions to help you in your spiritual life. It is hoped that the book will serve as an instrument of devotional inspiration as well as a guide for worship. It will assist us as we reach out to spread the Gospel of Jesus Christ.

The development of this particular edition began with an assessment of the devotional and spiritual needs of persons serving in the military and in Veterans Administration Medical Centers. I am particularly grateful to Howard E. Galley who, with the Rev. Dr. Donald W. Beers, compiled and edited this book. Thanks are also due to the Rev. Dr. Herbert Arrunategui who assisted with the Spanish portions of the book.

May God continue to guide us as we offer ourselves to Him and to each other.

✠ Charles L. Keyser
IV SUFFRAGAN BISHOP FOR THE ARMED FORCES

FOREWORD

To all who serve our country:

This Prayer Book for the Armed Forces serves as one symbol of the Episcopal Church's commitment to its ministry to all who serve our country. Other manifestations of our commitment include the Suffragan Bishop for the Armed Forces, the chaplains on active and reserve duty, and the clergy and lay persons of our many congregations who minister to the men and women of our armed forces.

This Prayer Book will hopefully nurture your spiritual life, which will in turn enable you not only to fulfill with dedication your responsibilities while on active duty, but also to nurture a deeper commitment to the Lord Jesus. In his Epistle to the Ephesians, St. Paul compares the armor of the soldier to the armor of God, a description of the spiritual disciplines and virtues of the committed Christian.

I pray that this gift to you may also serve as a reminder that through your baptism you are an integral part of the whole Body of Christ, the Church. In your vocation and ministry of service to our country, you are a part of the whole ministry and life of this Church.

May God's Peace and Blessing be with you always.

Faithfully in Christ,

✠ Edmond L. Browning
PRESIDING BISHOP

THE EPISCOPAL CHURCH SERVICE CROSS

The Episcopal Church Service Cross carries the design of the ancient Crusader's Cross, the five-fold cross symbolic of the five wounds of our Lord Jesus Christ at his crucifixion. The words embossed upon it, "Christ died for thee," are adapted from 2 Corinthians 5:15.

The Crusader's Cross was originally known as the Jerusalem Cross, incorporated in the coat-of-arms of the Latin Kingdom of Jerusalem in the 12th century as the coat-of-arms of Godfrey de Bouillon, first ruler of that kingdom. This Jerusalem Cross was carried on the shields, banners, and coats of the Crusaders from England, France, Germany, Italy, and Spain, and so became identified with them as the Crusader's Cross.

This cross is sometimes used as the emblem of missionary work, the large center cross representing the original Church in Jerusalem, and the smaller crosses indicating the "four corners of the earth" to which Christianity was spread through missionary endeavor.

The Service Cross was designed under the direction of Edith Weir Perry, wife of Bishop James De Wolf Perry, who was the Presiding Bishop of the Church from 1930 to 1937. The cross was first issued during World War I.

This cross is a distinct mark of an Episcopalian in the Armed Forces, and it is suggested that you wear it or carry it with you at all times.

Daily Devotions, Sacraments, and Services

DAILY DEVOTIONS

For hundreds of years, Christian people have lifted up their hearts to God in praise and prayer in the morning and again in the evening. The brief services which follow, taken from the Book of Common Prayer, are intended to help you share in the Church's prayer at these two times of the day. There are also forms, if you wish to use them, for prayer at noon and before going to sleep at night.

Each of these services may be used every day just as they are printed on the page. You may, however, substitute other Psalms, Readings, and Collects for those printed in the services. A table of suggested Psalms for morning and evening is on page 7. Alternative Readings and Collects are given on pages 8-17. One of the hymns on pages 132-152 may be used in place of "O gracious Light" on page 5. Any or all of these alternatives may be used, as desired.

When these forms are used by families, or by two or more people, the Reading and Collect should be read by one person. Other parts may be said by all together.

For these same devotions in Spanish, see pages 18-21.

On Sundays, if you cannot attend a service of worship, it is suggested that, in addition to your daily prayers, you use the devotions suggested on page 55.

In the Morning

From Psalm 51

Open my lips, O Lord,*
   and my mouth shall proclaim your praise.
Create in me a clean heart, O God,*
   and renew a right spirit within me.
Cast me not away from your presence*
   and take not your holy Spirit from me.
Give me the joy of your saving help again*
   and sustain me with your bountiful Spirit.
Glory to the Father, and to the Son, and to the Holy Spirit:*
   as it was in the beginning, is now, and will be for ever. Amen.

A Reading

Blessed be the God and Father of our Lord Jesus Christ!
By his great mercy we have been born anew to a living hope
through the resurrection of Jesus Christ from the dead.   *1 Peter 1:3*

A period of silence may follow.

A hymn or canticle may be used. (See pages 90-91 and 131.)

The Apostles' Creed may be said. (See inside front cover.)

Prayers may be offered for ourselves and others.

The Lord's Prayer

The Collect

Lord God, almighty and everlasting Father, you have brought us
in safety to this new day: Preserve us with your mighty power,
that we may not fall into sin, nor be overcome by adversity; and
in all we do, direct us to the fulfilling of your purpose; through
Jesus Christ our Lord. *Amen.*

At Noon

From Psalm 113

Give praise, you servants of the LORD;*
  praise the Name of the LORD.
Let the Name of the LORD be blessed,*
  from this time forth for evermore.
From the rising of the sun to its going down*
  let the Name of the LORD be praised.
The LORD is high above all nations,*
  and his glory above the heavens.
Glory to the Father, and to the Son, and to the Holy Spirit:*
  as it was in the beginning, is now, and will be for ever. Amen.

A Reading

O God, you will keep in perfect peace those whose minds are
fixed on you; for in returning and rest we shall be saved; in quietness and trust shall be our strength.   *Isaiah 26:3; 30:15*

Prayers may be offered for ourselves and others.

The Lord's Prayer

The Collect

Blessed Savior, at this hour you hung upon the cross, stretching
out your loving arms: Grant that all the peoples of the earth may
look to you and be saved; for your mercies' sake. *Amen.*

or this

Lord Jesus Christ, you said to your apostles, "Peace I give to you;
my own peace I leave with you:" Regard not our sins, but the
faith of your Church, and give to us the peace and unity of that
heavenly City, where with the Father and the Holy Spirit you live
and reign, now and for ever. *Amen.*

In the Early Evening

This devotion may be used before or after the evening meal.

O gracious Light,
pure brightness of the everliving Father in heaven,
O Jesus Christ, holy and blessed!

Now as we come to the setting of the sun,
and our eyes behold the vesper light,
we sing your praises O God: Father, Son, and Holy Spirit.

You are worthy at all times to be praised by happy voices,
O Son of God, O Giver of life,
and to be glorified through all the worlds.

One or two Psalms may be said. (See page 7.)

A Reading
It is not ourselves that we proclaim; we proclaim Christ Jesus as
Lord, and ourselves as your servants, for Jesus' sake. For the
same God who said, "Out of darkness let light shine," has caused
his light to shine within us, to give the light of revelation—the
revelation of the glory of God in the face of Jesus Christ.
2 Corinthians 4:5-6

A canticle or hymn may be said. (See pages 92 and 131.)

Prayers may be offered for ourselves and others.

The Lord's Prayer

The Collect
Lord Jesus, stay with us, for evening is at hand and the day is
past; be our companion in the way, kindle our hearts, and awaken
hope, that we may know you as you are revealed in Scripture and
the breaking of bread. Grant this for the sake of your love. *Amen.*

At the Close of Day

Psalm 134

Behold now, bless the LORD, all you servants of the LORD,*
  you that stand by night in the house of the LORD.
Lift up your hands in the holy place and bless the LORD;*
  the LORD who made heaven and earth bless you out of Zion.
Glory to the Father, and to the Son, and to the Holy Spirit:*
  as it was in the beginning, is now, and will be for ever. Amen.

A Reading

Lord, you are in the midst of us and we are called by your Name:
Do not forsake us, O Lord our God.   *Jeremiah 14:9,22*

The following canticle or a hymn may be said

The Song of Simeon

Lord, you now have set your servant free*
  to go in peace as you have promised;
For these eyes of mine have seen the Savior,*
  whom you have prepared for all the world to see:
A Light to enlighten the nations,*
  and the glory of your people Israel.

*Prayers for ourselves and others may follow. It is appropriate that prayers
of thanksgiving for the blessings of the day, and penitence for our sins, be
included.*

The Lord's Prayer

The Collect

Visit this place, O Lord, and drive far from it all snares of the
enemy; let your holy angels dwell with us to preserve us in peace;
and let your blessing be upon us always; through Jesus Christ our
Lord. *Amen.*

The almighty and merciful Lord, Father, Son, and Holy Spirit,
bless us and keep us. *Amen.*

A TABLE OF PSALMS

The following Psalms are appropriate for use in Daily Devotions at the times indicated. The Psalms are on pages 74-90.

	Morning	*Evening*
Sunday	95, 146	98, 114
	or	
	118, 150	
Monday	1, 121	46
Tuesday	63, 67	84
Wednesday	51	103
Thursday	65	85, 130
Friday	22	139
In Easter Season:	95, 146	
Saturday	24, 100	23, 122

Christmas Eve		67, 100
Christmas Day	98, 150	85, 146
	These same psalms may also be used on New Year's Eve and Day.	
Epiphany	85, 146	67, 100
Sundays in Lent	63, 98	103
Sundays of Easter	118, 150	98, 114
Ascension Day	24, 150	98, 100
All Saints' Day	98, 150	46
Other Feasts	95, 98	46 *or* 84
Thanksgiving Day	65	67, 100
Other National Days	98, 146	67, 100

READINGS AND COLLECTS

Any of the following Bible Readings and Collects may be used in place of those given in the forms for Daily Devotion, pages 3-6.

Know this day, and lay it to your heart, that the Lord is God in heaven above and on the earth beneath; there is no other.
Deuteronomy 4:39.

Fear not, for I am with you, be not dismayed, for I am your God; I will strengthen you, I will help you, I will uphold you with my victorious right hand.   *Isaiah 41:10.*

Jesus said, "Come to me, all who labor and are heavy laden, and I will give you rest. Take my yoke upon you, and learn from me; for I am gentle and lowly in heart, and you will find rest for your souls. For my yoke is easy, and my burden is light."
Matthew 11:28-30.

God so loved the world that he gave his only Son, that whoever believes in him should not perish but have eternal life. For God sent the Son into the world, not to condemn the world, but that the world might be saved through him.   *John 3:16-17.*

Jesus said, "I am the light of the world; whoever follows me will not walk in darkness, but will have the light of life."   *John 8:12.*

Since we are justified by faith, we have peace with God through our Lord Jesus Christ.   *Romans 5:1.*

The fruit of the Spirit is love, joy, peace, patience, kindness, goodness, faithfulness, gentleness, self-control.   *Galatians 5:22-23a.*

There is one body and one Spirit, just as you were called to the one hope that belongs to your call, one Lord, one faith, one baptism, one God and Father of us all, who is above all and through all and in all.   *Ephesians 4:4-6.*

Whatever you do, in word or deed, do everything in the name of the Lord Jesus, giving thanks to God the Father through him.
Colossians 3:17.

Count it all joy when you meet various trials, for you know that the testing of your faith produces steadfastness. And let steadfastness have its full effect, that you may be perfect and complete, lacking in nothing. *James 1:2-4.*

In this the love of God was made manifest among us: that God sent his only Son into the world, so that we might live through him. *1 John 4:9.*

A Reading for Fridays
I have been crucified with Christ; it is no longer I who live, but Christ who lives in me; and the life I now live in the flesh I live by faith in the Son of God, who loved me and gave himself for me. *Galatians 2:20.*

A Morning Collect
O God, the King eternal, whose light divides the day from the night and turns the shadow of death into the morning: Drive far from us all wrong desires, incline our hearts to keep your law, and guide our feet into the way of peace; that, having done your will with cheerfulness during the day, we may, when night comes, rejoice to give you thanks; through Jesus Christ our Lord. *Amen.*

An Evening Collect
O God, the life of all who live, the light of the faithful, the strength of those who labor, and the repose of the dead: We thank you for the blessings of the day that is past, and humbly ask for your protection through the coming night. Bring us in safety to the morning hours; through him who died and rose again for us, your Son our Savior Jesus Christ. *Amen.*

A Collect for Fridays
Almighty God, whose most dear Son went not up to joy but first he suffered pain, and entered not into glory before he was crucified: Mercifully grant that we, walking in the way of the cross, may find it none other than the way of life and peace; through Jesus Christ your Son our Lord. *Amen.*

SUNDAY MORNING

Reading

Blessing and glory and wisdom and thanksgiving and honor and power and might be to our God for ever and ever! Amen.
Revelation 7:12.

Collect

O God our King, by the resurrection of your Son Jesus Christ on the first day of the week, you conquered sin, put death to flight, and gave us the hope of everlasting life: Redeem all our days by this victory; forgive our sins, banish our fears, make us bold to praise you and to do your will; and steel us to wait for the consummation of your kingdom on the last great Day; through the same Jesus Christ our Lord. *Amen.*

SUNDAY EVENING

Reading

Blessed be the God and Father of our Lord Jesus Christ, the Father of mercies and God of all comfort, who comforts us in all our affliction. *2 Corinthians 1:3-4a.*

Collect

Lord God, whose Son our Savior Jesus Christ triumphed over the powers of death and prepared for us our place in the new Jerusalem: Grant that we, who have this day given thanks for his resurrection, may praise you in that City of which he is the light, and where he lives and reigns for ever and ever. *Amen.*

FOR THE CHURCH YEAR

When two Readings are given, one may be used in the morning and the other in the evening. See page 153 for an explanation of the Church Year.

ADVENT

(The four weeks before Christmas)

In the wilderness prepare the way of the Lord, make straight in the desert a highway for our God. *Isaiah 40:3.*

Jesus said, "Watch, for you do not know when the master of the house will come, in the evening, or at midnight, or at cockcrow, or in the morning—lest he come suddenly and find you asleep."
Mark 13:35-36.

Collect
Almighty God, give us grace to cast away the works of darkness, and put on the armor of light, now in the time of this mortal life in which your Son Jesus Christ came to visit us in great humility; that in the last day, when he shall come again in his glorious majesty to judge both the living and the dead, we may rise to the life immortal; through him who lives and reigns with you and the Holy Spirit, one God, now and for ever. *Amen.*

CHRISTMAS

(December 25 until January 6)

To us a child is born, to us a son is given; and the government will be upon his shoulder, and his name will be called "Wonderful Counselor, Mighty God, Everlasting Father, Prince of Peace." *Isaiah 9:6.*

Behold, the dwelling of God is with humankind. He will dwell with them, and they shall be his people, and God himself will be with them, and be their God. *Revelation 21:3.*

For the Christmas story, see page 104, no. 11.

Collect
Almighty God, you have given your only-begotten Son to take our nature upon him, and to be born [this day] of a pure virgin: Grant that we, who have been born again and made your children by adoption and grace, may daily be renewed by your Holy Spirit; through our Lord Jesus Christ, to whom with you and the same Spirit be honor and glory, now and for ever. *Amen.*

EPIPHANY

(January 6 through the following Saturday evening)

Arise, shine; for your light has come, and the glory of the Lord has risen upon you. *Isaiah 60:1.*

Collect
O God, by the leading of a star you manifested your only Son to the peoples of the earth: Lead us, who know you now by faith, to your presence, where we may see your glory face to face; through Jesus Christ our Lord, who lives and reigns with you and the Holy Spirit, one God, now and for ever. *Amen.*

On Sundays after Epiphany, use the Readings and Collects for Sundays, page 10.

LENT
(Ash Wednesday until Palm Sunday)

Rend your hearts and not your garments. Return to the Lord your God, for he is gracious and merciful, slow to anger and abounding in steadfast love, and repents of evil. *Joel 2:13.*

If we say we have no sin, we deceive ourselves, and the truth is not in us, but if we confess our sins, God, who is faithful and just will forgive our sins and cleanse us from all unrighteousness. *1 John 1:8-9.*

Reading for Sundays in Lent
Remember Jesus Christ, risen from the dead. The saying is sure: If we have died with him, we shall also live with him; if we endure, we shall also reign with him; if we deny him, he also will deny us; if we are faithless, he remains faithful — for he cannot deny himself. *2 Timothy 2:8a, 11-13.*

Collect
Almighty and everlasting God, you hate nothing you have made and forgive the sins of all who are penitent: Create and make in us new and contrite hearts, that we, worthily lamenting our sins and acknowledging our wretchedness, may obtain of you, the God of all mercy, perfect remission and forgiveness; through Jesus Christ our Lord, who lives and reigns with you and the Holy Spirit, one God, for ever and ever. *Amen.*

HOLY WEEK
(Palm Sunday through Holy Saturday)

He was wounded for our transgressions, he was bruised for our iniquities; upon him was the chastisement that made us whole, and with his stripes we are healed. All we like sheep have gone astray; we have turned every one to his own way; and the Lord has laid on him the iniquity of us all. *Isaiah 53:5-6.*

Christ died for sins once for all, the righteous for the unrighteous, that he might bring us to God. *1 Peter 3:18a.*

For the story of Christ's death, see page 109, no. 26.

Collect

Almighty and everliving God, in your tender love for the human race you sent your Son our Savior Jesus Christ to take upon him our nature, and to suffer death upon the cross, giving us the example of his great humility: Mercifully grant that we may walk in the way of his suffering, and also share in his resurrection; through Jesus Christ our Lord, who lives and reigns with you and the Holy Spirit, one God, for ever and ever. *Amen.*

EASTER
(Easter Day until Ascension Day)

Thanks be to God who gives us the victory through our Lord Jesus Christ. *1 Corinthians 15:57.*

You are a chosen race, a royal priesthood, a holy nation, God's own people, that you may declare the wonderful deeds of him who called you out of darkness into his marvelous light. *1 Peter 2:9.*

For the Easter story, see pages 109-110, nos. 27 and 28.

Collect

O God, who for our redemption gave your only-begotten Son to the death of the cross, and by his glorious resurrection delivered us from the power of our enemy: Grant us so to die daily to sin, that we may evermore live with him in the joy of his resurrection; through Jesus Christ your Son our Lord, who lives and reigns with you and the Holy Spirit, one God, now and for ever. *Amen.*

ASCENSION
(Ascension Day until Day of Pentecost)

Christ has entered, not into a sanctuary made with hands, a copy of the true one, but into heaven itself, now to appear in the presence of God on our behalf. *Hebrews 9:24.*

Since you have been raised with Christ, seek the things that are above, where Christ is, seated at the right hand of God. *Colossians 3:1.*

For the story of the Ascension, see page 110, no. 30.

Collect

Almighty God, whose blessed Son our Savior Jesus Christ ascended far above all heavens that he might fill all things: Mercifully give us faith to perceive that, according to his promise, he abides with his Church on earth, even to the end of the ages; through Jesus Christ our Lord, who lives and reigns with you and the Holy Spirit, one God, in glory everlasting. *Amen.*

THE DAY OF PENTECOST

God's love has been poured into our hearts through the Holy Spirit which has been given to us. *Romans 5:5.*

For the story of Pentecost, see page 111, no. 31.

Collect

Almighty God, on this day you opened the way of eternal life to every race and nation by the promised gift of your Holy Spirit: Shed abroad this gift throughout the world by the preaching of the Gospel, that it may reach to the ends of the earth; through Jesus Christ our Lord, who lives and reigns with you, in the unity of the Holy Spirit, one God, for ever and ever. *Amen.*

TRINITY SUNDAY
(The first Sunday after Pentecost)

Holy, holy, holy, is the Lord God Almighty, who was and is and is to come! *Revelation 4:8.*

Collect

Almighty and everlasting God, you have given to us your servants grace, by the confession of a true faith, to acknowledge the glory of the eternal Trinity, and in the power of your divine Majesty to worship the Unity: Keep us steadfast in this faith and worship, and bring us at last to see you in your one and eternal glory, O Father; who with the Son and the Holy Spirit live and reign, one God, for ever and ever. *Amen.*

On other Sundays after Pentecost, use the Readings and Collects for Sundays, page 10.

ALL SAINTS' DAY

I beheld a great multitude which no one could count, from all nations and tribes and peoples and tongues, standing before the throne and before the Lamb, clothed in white robes and with palms in their hands, and crying out with a loud voice, "Salvation belongs to our God who sits upon the throne and to the Lamb!"
Revelation 7:9-10

Collect

Almighty God, you have knit together your elect in one communion and fellowship in the mystical body of your Son Christ our Lord: Give us grace so to follow your blessed saints in all virtuous and godly living, that we may come to those ineffable joys that you have prepared for those who truly love you; through Jesus Christ our Lord, who with you and the Holy Spirit lives and reigns, one God, in glory everlasting. *Amen.*

FEASTS OF OUR LORD DURING THE YEAR
(Feasts as indicated by the symbol [†] on pages 154-155)

Great indeed is the mystery of our religion: He was manifested in the flesh, vindicated in the Spirit, seen by angels, preached among the nations, believed on in the world, taken up in glory.
1 Timothy 3:16.

The Word became flesh and dwelt among us, full of grace and truth; we have beheld his glory, glory as of the only Son from the Father. *John 1:14.*

Collect

Almighty God, you have poured upon us the new light of your incarnate Word: Grant that this light, enkindled in our hearts, may shine forth in our lives; through Jesus Christ our Lord, who lives and reigns with you, in the unity of the Holy Spirit, one God, now and for ever. *Amen.*

FEASTS OF APOSTLES
(See the list of holy days on pages 154-155)

Those who were baptized devoted themselves to the apostles' teaching and fellowship, to the breaking of bread and the prayers. *Acts 2:42*

The gifts of Christ were that some should be apostles, some prophets, some evangelists, some pastors and teachers, to equip the saints for the work of ministry, for the building up of the body of Christ. *Ephesians 4:11-12*

Collect

Almighty God, you have built your Church upon the foundation of the apostles and prophets, Jesus Christ himself being the chief cornerstone: Grant us so to be joined together in unity of spirit by their teaching, that we may be made a holy temple acceptable to you; through Jesus Christ our Lord, who lives and reigns with you and the Holy Spirit, one God, for ever and ever. *Amen.*

OTHER SAINTS' DAYS
(See the list of holy days on pages 154-155)

We give thanks to the Father, who has made us worthy to share in the inheritance of the saints in light. *Colossians 1:12.*

You are no longer strangers and sojourners, but fellow citizens with the saints and members of the household of God.
Ephesians 2:19.

Collect

Almighty God, by your Holy Spirit you have made us one with your saints in heaven and on earth: Grant that in our earthly pilgrimage we may always be supported by this fellowship of love and prayer, and know ourselves to be surrounded by their witness to your power and mercy. We ask this for the sake of Jesus Christ, in whom all our intercessions are acceptable through the Spirit, and who lives and reigns for ever and ever.   *Amen.*

or this

Almighty God, you have surrounded us with a great cloud of witnesses: Grant that we, encouraged by the good example of your servant *N.*, may persevere in running the race that is set before us, until at last we may with *him* attain to your eternal joy;

through Jesus Christ, the pioneer and perfecter of our faith, who lives and reigns with you and the Holy Spirit, one God, for ever and ever. *Amen.*

NATIONAL DAYS

Give thanks to the Lord, call upon his name; make known his deeds among the nations, proclaim that his Name is exalted.
Isaiah 12:4b.

Collect
Lord God Almighty, in whose Name the founders of this country won liberty for themselves and for us, and lit the torch of freedom for nations then unborn: Grant that we and all the people of this land may have grace to maintain our liberties in righteousness and peace; through Jesus Chirst our Lord, who lives and reigns with you and the Holy Spirit, one God, for ever and ever. *Amen.*

Por la Mañana

Del Salmo 51
Señor, abre mis labios,*
    y mi boca proclamará tu alabanza.
Crea en mí, oh Dios, un corazón limpio,*
    y renueva un espíritu firme dentro de mí.
No me eches de tu presencia,*
    y no quites de mí tu santo Espíritu.
Dame otra vez el gozo de tu salvación;*
    y que tu noble Espíritu me sustente.
Gloria al Padre, y al Hijo y al Espíritu Santo:*
    como era en el principio, ahora y siempre,
    por los siglos de los siglos. Amén.

Lectura
Bendito el Dios y Padre de nuestro Señor Jesucristo, que
según su grande misericordia nos hizo renacer para una
esperanza viva, por la resurrección de Jesucristo de los
muertos.   *1 San Pedro 1:3*

Puede seguir un período de silencio.

Puede usarse un himno o cántico.

Puede decirse el Credo de los Apóstoles.
    (Vea dentro de la cubierta de atrás.)

Puede ofrecerse plegarias por nosotros mismos y por los demás.

El Padre Nuestro

Colecta
Señor Dios, todopoderoso y eterno Padre, nos hiciste
llegar sanos y salvos hasta este nuevo día: Consérvanos
con tu gran poder, para que no caigamos en pecado, ni
no venza la adversidad; y, en todo lo que hagamos,
dirígenos a realizar tus designios; por Jesucristo nuestro
Señor. *Amén.*

Al Mediodía

Del Salmo 113

Alaben las obras del Señor;*
    alaben el Nombre del Señor.
Sea bendito el Nombre del Señor,*
    desde ahora y para siempre.
Desde el nacimiento del sol hasta donde se pone,*
    sea alabado el Nombre del Señor.
Excelso sobre todas las naciones es el Señor,*
    sobre los cielos su gloria.
Gloria al Padre, y al Hijo y al Espíritu Santo:*
    como era en el principio, ahora y siempre,
    por los siglos de los siglos. Amén.

Lectura

Oh Dios, tú guardarás en completa paz a aquél cuyo
pensamiento en ti persevera; porque en descanso y en
reposo seremos salvos; en quietud y en confianza será
nuestra fortaleza.   *Isaias 26:3; 30:15*

Puede ofrecerse plegarias por nosotros mismos y por los demás.

El Padre Nuestro

Colecta

Bendito Salvador, en esta hora colgabas en la cruz,
extendiendo tus brazos amorosos: Concede que todos los
pueblos de la tierra miren hacia ti y sean salvos; por tu
entrañable misericordia. *Amén.*

o bien:

Señor Jesucristo, que dijiste a tus apóstoles, "La paz les
dejo, mi paz les doy": No mires nuestros pecados sino la
fe de tu Iglesia: y concédenos la paz y la unidad de esa
Ciudad celestial; donde con el Padre y el Espíritu Santo
tú vives y reinas ahora y por siempre. *Amén.*

Al Atardecer

Esta devoción puede usarse antes o después de la cena.

Luz alegrante,
claridad pura del sempiterno Padre celestial,
Jesucristo, santo y bendito:

Ahora que hemos llegado al ocaso del sol,
y nuestros ojos miran la luz vespertina,
te alabamos con himnos, oh Dios: Padre,
    Hijo y Espíritu Santo.

Digno eres de ser alabado en todos los tiempos
    con voces gozosas,
oh Hijo de Dios, Dador de la vida;
    por tanto te glorifica el universo entero.

Uno o dos salmos pueden ser recitados. (Vea páginas 93-96.)

Lectura

No nos predicamos a nosotros mismos, sino a Jesucristo
como Señor, y a nosotros como siervos de ustedes por
amor de Jesús. Porque Dios, que mandó que de las
tinieblas resplandeciese la luz, es el que resplandeció en
nuestros corazones, para iluminación del conocimiento
de la gloria de Dios en la faz de Jesucristo.
2 Corintios 4:5-6

Puede ofrecerse plegarias por nosotros mismos y por los demás.

El Padre Nuestro

Colecta

Quédate con nosotros, Señor Jesús, ahora que la noche se
acerca y ha pasado el día. Sé nuestro compañero en el
camino, enciende nuestros corazones, y despierta la
esperanza, para que te conozcamos tal como te revelas en
las Escrituras y en la fracción del pan. Concede esto por
amor de tu Nombre. *Amén.*

Al Terminar el Día

Salmo 134

Y ahora bendigan al Señor,
siervos todos del Señor,*
   los que de noche están de pie en la casa del Señor.
Eleven las manos hacia el santuario,
y bendigan al Señor.*
   El Señor que hizo los cielos y la tierra,
   te bendiga desde Sión.

Lectura

Tú estás entre nosotros, oh Señor, y sobre nosotros es
invocado tu Nombre; no nos desampares, Señor nuestro
Dios.   *Jeremías 14:9, 22*

Puede decirse lo siguiente:
Cántico de Simeón

Ahora despides, Señor, a tu siervo,*
   conforme a tu palabra, en paz;
Porque mis ojos han visto a tu Salvador,*
   a quien has presentato ante todos los pueblos;
Luz para alumbrar a las naciones,*
   y gloria de tu pueblo Israel.

*Pueden seguir plegarias por nosotros mismos y por los demás. Es
apropiado que se incluyan oraciones de acción de gracias por las
bendiciones del día, y de penitencia por nuestros pecados.*

El Padre Nuestro

Colecta

Visita, oh Señor, este lugar, y ahuyenta de él todas las
asechanzas del enemigo; que tus santos ángeles moren
con nosotros para preservarnos en paz; y que tu
bendición sea siempre sobre nosotros; por Jesucristo
nuestro Señor. *Amén.*

Que el Señor omnipotente y misericordioso: Padre, Hijo
y Espíritu Santo, nos bendiga y nos guarde. *Amén.*

A SERVICE OF WORSHIP

This service may be led by a chaplain or lay reader. In the absence of such a person, any Christian may lead this service.

Whenever possible, the leader should appoint other persons to read the Scripture Readings which precede the Gospel and to lead the Prayers of the People.

When circumstances permit, hymns should be sung at the places indicated. When necessary, however, they may be omitted.

The Scripture Readings should ordinarily be those appointed in the Lectionary of the Book of Common Prayer (or in the similar lectionary in the *Book of Worship for United States Forces*). When necessary, however, Readings from this book may be used instead. For suggested Readings, see page 99. For Psalms, see page 73. For hymns, see page 131.

If a shorter form of service is desired, one of the first two Readings may be omitted. In that case, the Psalm follows the Reading chosen.

If all do not have books, a member of the congregation may be appointed to read the Psalm.

When the service is led by a chaplain, a sermon may follow the Gospel and the service may end with a priestly blessing. A licensed lay reader may read an authorized sermon. A chaplain or lay reader may also, instead of using this form of service, use the Liturgy of the Word from the Holy Eucharist, concluding it as indicated at the top of page 43.

ORDER OF THE SERVICE

1. Opening Hymn.

2. Opening Prayer. *The leader may use one of the Collects on pages 10-17, or some other prayer.*

3. First Reading. *From the Old Testament. In Easter Season it is customary to read from the Acts of the Apostles instead.*

4. Psalm. *Said by all together.*

5. Second Reading. *From any New Testament book except the Gospels.*

6. Hymn.

7. Gospel. *All stand for this reading.*

8. Response to the Gospel. *The leader, or some other person, may comment briefly on the Gospel passage. Alternatively, all may meditate on the passage, sitting in silence.*

9. Creed. *Either the Apostles' Creed (inside front cover) or the Nicene Creed (page 39) may be said, or the Creed may be omitted.*

10. Prayers of the People. *One of the forms on pages 40-42 may be used, or other prayers may be said.*

11. The Lord's Prayer. *Said by all together.*

12. Closing Hymn.

The leader ends the service with one of the blessings on page 127 or with the following

The grace of our Lord Jesus Christ, and the love of God, and the fellowship of the Holy Spirit, be with us all evermore. *Amen.*
2 Corinthians 13:14.

ABOUT HOLY BAPTISM

Holy Baptism is the sacrament by which we are born again by water and the Spirit. In this sacrament God adopts us as his children, unites us to Christ in his death and resurrection, makes us members of Christ's Body the Church, forgives our sins, and gives us new life in the Holy Spirit.

Ordinarily, Baptism is administered at a celebration of the Holy Eucharist, especially on Easter Day, or on some other Sunday or feast day.

The Episcopal Church, like most churches, recognizes all Baptisms reverently performed with water in the Name of the Father, and of the Son, and of the Holy Spirit.

Adults desiring to be baptized should speak to the chaplain as soon as possible, in order that they may receive instruction in the Christian faith. They should also prepare themselves by repentance and prayer to receive this holy Sacrament.

When the Bishop is present at Baptism, it is he who performs the Laying on of Hands (and anointing) that follows the administration of the water. Adults who receive this Laying on of Hands by the Bishop do not need to be confirmed later.

The service of Holy Baptism is the usual time for the Bishop to administer Confirmation and to receive persons baptized in some other Church into the Episcopal Church. It is also the time when persons who have abandoned the practice of the Christian religion may reaffirm their baptismal vows and be welcomed back by the Bishop.

For the form for Emergency Baptism, see pages 34-35.

Will you be responsible for seeing that the child you present is brought up in the Christian faith and life?

Parents and Godparents

I will, with God's help.

Celebrant

Will you by your prayers and witness help this child to grow into the full stature of Christ?

Parents and Godparents

I will, with God's help.

Then the Celebrant asks the following questions of the candidates who can speak for themselves, and of the parents and godparents who speak on behalf of the infants and younger children

Question Do you renounce Satan and all the spiritual forces of wickedness that rebel against God?

Answer I renounce them.

Question Do you renounce the evil powers of this world which corrupt and destroy the creatures of God?

Answer I renounce them.

Question Do you renounce all sinful desires that draw you from the love of God?

Answer I renounce them.

Question Do you turn to Jesus Christ and accept him as your Savior?

Answer I do.

Question Do you put your whole trust in his grace and love?
Answer I do.

Question Do you promise to follow and obey him as your Lord?
Answer I do.

When there are others to be presented, the Bishop says

The other Candidate(s) will now be presented.

Presenters I present *these persons* for Confirmation.

or I present *these persons* to be received into this Communion.

or I present *these persons* who *desire* to reaffirm *their* baptismal vows.

The Bishop asks the candidates

Do you reaffirm your renunciation of evil?

Candidate I do.

Bishop

Do you renew your commitment to Jesus Christ?

Candidate

I do, and with God's grace I will follow him as my Savior and Lord.

After all have been presented, the Celebrant addresses the congregation, saying

Will you who witness these vows do all in your power to support *these persons* in *their* life in Christ?

People We will.

The Celebrant then says these or similar words

Let us join with *those* who *are* committing *themselves* to Christ and renew our own baptismal covenant.

The Baptismal Covenant

Celebrant Do you believe in God the Father?

People I believe in God, the Father almighty,
  creator of heaven and earth.

Celebrant Do you believe in Jesus Christ, the Son of God?

People I believe in Jesus Christ, his only Son, our Lord.
  He was conceived by the power of the Holy Spirit
    and born of the Virgin Mary.
  He suffered under Pontius Pilate,
    was crucified, died, and was buried.
  He descended to the dead.
  On the third day he rose again.
  He ascended into heaven,
    and is seated at the right hand of the Father.
  He will come again to judge the living and the dead.

Celebrant Do you believe in God the Holy Spirit?

People I believe in the Holy Spirit,
  the holy catholic Church,

the communion of saints,
the forgiveness of sins,
the resurrection of the body,
and the life everlasting.

Celebrant Will you continue in the apostles' teaching and
fellowship, in the breaking of bread, and in the
prayers?

People I will, with God's help.

Celebrant Will you persevere in resisting evil, and, whenever
you fall into sin, repent and return to the Lord?

People I will, with God's help.

Celebrant Will you proclaim by word and example the Good
News of God in Christ?

People I will, with God's help.

Celebrant Will you seek and serve Christ in all persons, loving
your neighbor as yourself?

People I will, with God's help.

Celebrant Will you strive for justice and peace among all
people, and respect the dignity of every human
being?

People I will, with God's help.

Prayers for the Candidates

The Celebrant then says to the congregation

Let us now pray for *these persons* who *are* to receive the
Sacrament of new birth [and for those (this person) who *have*
renewed *their* commitment to Christ.]

A Person appointed leads the following petitions

Leader Deliver *them,* O Lord, from the way of sin and death.

People Lord, hear our prayer.

Leader Open *their hearts* to your grace and truth.

People Lord, hear our prayer.

Leader Keep *them* in the faith and communion of your holy
Church.

People Lord, hear our prayer.

Leader	Teach *them* to love others in the power of the Spirit.
People	Lord, hear our prayer.
Leader	Send *them* into the world in witness to your love.
People	Lord, hear our prayer.
Leader	Bring *them* to the fullness of your peace and glory.
People	Lord, hear our prayer.

The Celebrant says

Grant, O Lord, that all who are baptized into the death of Jesus Christ your Son may live in the power of his resurrection and look for him to come again in glory; who lives and reigns now and for ever. *Amen.*

Thanksgiving over the Water

The Celebrant blesses the water, first saying

	The Lord be with you.
People	And also with you.
Celebrant	Let us give thanks to the Lord our God.
People	It is right to give him thanks and praise.

Celebrant

We thank you, Almighty God, for the gift of water.
Over it the Holy Spirit moved in the beginning of creation.
Through it you led the children of Israel out of their bondage
in Egypt into the land of promise. In it your Son Jesus
received the baptism of John and was anointed by the Holy
Spirit as the Messiah, the Christ, to lead us, through his death
and resurrection, from the bondage of sin into everlasting life.

We thank you, Father, for the water of Baptism. In it we are
buried with Christ in his death. By it we share in his
resurrection. Through it we are reborn by the Holy Spirit.
Therefore in joyful obedience to your Son, we bring into his
fellowship those who come to him in faith, baptizing them in
the Name of the Father, and of the Son, and of the Holy Spirit.

At the following words, the Celebrant touches the water

Now sanctify this water, we pray you, by the power of your
Holy Spirit, that those who here are cleansed from sin and
born again may continue for ever in the risen life of Jesus
Christ our Savior.

To him, to you, and to the Holy Spirit, be all honor and
glory, now and for ever. *Amen.*

Consecration of the Chrism

*The Bishop may then consecrate oil of Chrism, placing a hand on the
vessel of oil, and saying*

Eternal Father, whose blessed Son was anointed by the
Holy Spirit to be the Savior and servant of all, we pray you to
consecrate this oil, that those who are sealed with it may
share in the royal priesthood of Jesus Christ; who lives and
reigns with you and the Holy Spirit, for ever and ever. *Amen.*

The Baptism

*Each candidate is presented by name to the Celebrant, or to an assisting
priest or deacon, who then immerses, or pours water upon, the candidate,
saying*

N., I baptize you in the Name of the Father, and of the Son, and
of the Holy Spirit. *Amen.*

*When this action has been completed for all candidates, the Bishop or
Priest, at a place in full sight of the congregation, prays over them, saying*

Let us pray.

Heavenly Father, we thank you that by water and the Holy Spirit
you have bestowed upon *these* your *servants* the forgiveness of
sin, and have raised *them* to the new life of grace. Sustain *them*,
O Lord, in your Holy Spirit. Give *them* an inquiring and discern-
ing heart, the courage to will and to persevere, a spirit to know
and to love you, and the gift of joy and wonder in all your works.
Amen.

Then the Bishop or Priest places a hand on the person's head, marking on the forehead the sign of the cross [using Chrism if desired] and saying to each one

N., you are sealed by the Holy Spirit in Baptism and marked as Christ's own for ever. *Amen.*

Or this action may be done immediately after the administration of the water and before the preceding prayer.

When all have been baptized, the Celebrant says

Let us welcome the newly baptized.

Celebrant and People

We receive you into the household of God. Confess the faith of Christ crucified, proclaim his resurrection, and share with us in his eternal priesthood.

If Confirmation, Reception, or the Reaffirmation of Baptismal Vows is not to follow, the Peace is now exchanged

Celebrant The peace of the Lord be always with you.

People   And also with you.

At Confirmation, Reception, or Reaffirmation

The Bishop says to the congregation

Let us now pray for *these persons* who *have* renewed *their* commitment to Christ.

Silence may be kept.

Then the Bishop says

Almighty God, we thank you that by the death and resurrection of your Son Jesus Christ you have overcome sin and brought us to yourself, and that by the sealing of your Holy Spirit you have bound us to your service. Renew in *these* your *servants* the covenant you made with *them* at *their* Baptism. Send *them* forth in the power of that Spirit to perform the service you set before *them;* through Jesus Christ your Son our Lord, who lives and reigns with you and the Holy Spirit, one God, now and for ever. *Amen.*

For Confirmation

The Bishop lays hands upon each one and says

Strengthen, O Lord, your servant *N.* with your Holy Spirit; em-
power *him* for your service; and sustain *him* all the days of *his*
life. *Amen.*

or this

Defend, O Lord, your servant *N.* with your heavenly grace,
that *he* may continue yours for ever, and daily increase in your
Holy Spirit more and more, until *he* comes to your everlasting
kingdom. *Amen.*

For Reception

N., we recognize you as a member of the one holy catholic and
apostolic Church, and we receive you into the fellowship of this
Communion. God, the Father, Son, and Holy Spirit, bless,
preserve, and keep you. *Amen.*

For Reaffirmation

N., may the Holy Spirit, who has begun a good work in you,
direct and uphold you in the service of Christ and his kingdom.
Amen.

Then the Bishop says

Almighty and everliving God, let your fatherly hand ever be over
these your *servants;* let your Holy Spirit ever be with *them;* and
so lead *them* in the knowledge and obedience of your Word, that
they may serve you in this life, and dwell with you in the life to
come; through Jesus Christ our Lord. *Amen.*

The Peace is then exchanged

Bishop The peace of the Lord be always with you.
People And also with you.

At the Eucharist

The service then continues with the Prayers of the People or the Offertory of the Eucharist, at which the Bishop, when present, should be the principal Celebrant.

If there is no celebration of the Eucharist, the service concludes with the Lord's Prayer, a prayer by the celebrant, and a blessing.

Emergency Baptism

In case of emergency, any baptized person may administer Baptism according to the following form.

Using the given name of the one to be baptized (if known), pour water on him or her, saying

I baptize you in the Name of the Father, and of the Son, and of the Holy Spirit.

The Lord's Prayer is then said.

Other prayers, such as the following, may be added

Heavenly Father, we thank you that by water and the Holy Spirit you have bestowed upon this your servant the forgiveness of sin and have raised *him* to the new life of grace. Strengthen *him,* O Lord, with your presence, enfold *him* in the arms of your mercy, and keep *him* safe for ever.

If the newly baptized person is at the point of death, say this Commendation over him or her:

Depart, O Christian soul, out of this world;
In the Name of God the Father Almighty who created you;
In the Name of Jesus Christ who redeemed you;
In the Name of the Holy Spirit who sanctifies you.
May your rest be this day in peace,
    and your dwelling place in the Paradise of God.

Other prayers for the dying are on pages 64-69.

Report the facts to the chaplain when you can.

Bautismo en Caso de Emergencia

En caso de emergencia, cualquier persona bautizada puede administrar el Bautismo, de acuerdo con la siguiente fórmula.

Usando el nombre propio de la persona que va a ser bautizada (si se conoce), se derrama agua sobre la cabeza, diciendo:

Yo te bautizo en el Nombre del Padre, y del Hijo y del Espíritu Santo.

Después se dice el Padre Nuestro.

Pueden añadirse otras oraciones, como la siguiente:

Padre celestial, te damos gracias porque por medio del agua y del Espíritu Santo has concedido a este tu siervo el perdón de los pecados y le has levantado a la nueva vida de gracia. Fortalécele, oh Señor, con tu presencia, estréchale en los brazos du tu misericordia y protégele para siempre.

Si la persona que ha sido bautizada está agonizando, diga sobre ella la siguiente oración comendatoria:

Parte, oh alma cristiana, de este mundo;
En el nombre de Dios Padre todopoderoso, que te creó;
En el nombre de Jesucristo, que te redimió;
En el nombre del Espíritu Santo, que te santifica.
Que en este día, tu descanso sea en paz,
   y tu morada en el Paraíso de Dios.

Otras oraciones por los moribundos se encuentran en las páginas 64-69.

Informe al capellán de este hecho lo antes posible.

ABOUT THE HOLY EUCHARIST

The Holy Eucharist is the Church's principal act of worship on the Lord's Day (Sunday), on other great feast days, and on special occasions. The service consists of two major parts, the Ministry (or Liturgy) of the Word, in which we hear God's word read and preached; and the Celebration of the Holy Communion, in which we proclaim Christ's death and resurrection, and are united to him and to one another in the Sacrament of his Body and Blood.

In the Episcopal Church, the celebrant (presiding minister) at the Eucharist is always a bishop or priest. All baptized persons present, however, share in the celebration. In keeping with the teaching of Scripture, the elements used are bread and wine.

The Episcopal Church teaches that Christ is truly present at the Eucharist in accordance with his promise (Matthew 28:20). He is present in the midst of his people when they gather in his name, in the persons of the ministers who lead the service, in the reading and preaching of his word, and, in a special way, in the consecrated bread and wine (Matthew 18:20; Luke 24:30-35; John 6:53-56; 1 Corinthians 10:16-17). The Church does not try to explain Christ's presence in this sacrament, but it believes that it is a "real presence."

PREPARING FOR HOLY COMMUNION

It is the teaching of the Church, and of the New Testament, that those who come to the Eucharist should examine their lives, repent of their sins, and be in love and charity with all people. If you do not confess your sins and thank God for his blessings everyday in your prayers, it is especially important to do so before coming to Communion. In addition to praying in your own words, you may find it helpful to read some of the Psalms, Readings, and Prayers suggested on pages 73, 99, and 117 of this book. For further information about repentance, see page 59.

THE HOLY EUCHARIST: RITE TWO

The Word of God

A hymn, psalm, or anthem may be sung.

The people standing, the Celebrant says
> Blessed be God: Father, Son, and Holy Spirit.

People   And blessed be his kingdom, now and for ever. Amen.

In place of the above, from Easter Day through the Day of Pentecost
Celebrant   Alleluia. Christ is risen.
People   The Lord is risen indeed. Alleluia.

In Lent and on other penitential occasions
Celebrant   Bless the Lord who forgives all our sins.
People   His mercy endures for ever.

The Celebrant may say

Almighty God, to you all hearts are open, all desires known, and from you no secrets are hid: Cleanse the thoughts of our hearts by the inspiration of your Holy Spirit, that we may perfectly love you, and worthily magnify your holy Name; through Christ our Lord. *Amen.*

In place of the preceding prayer, the Confession of Sin on page 43 may be said.

When appointed, the following hymn or some other song of praise is sung or said, all standing

Glory to God in the highest,
    and peace to his people on earth.

Lord God, heavenly King,
almighty God and Father,
    we worship you, we give you thanks,
    we praise you for your glory.

Lord Jesus Christ, only Son of the Father,
Lord God, Lamb of God,
you take away the sin of the world:
    have mercy on us;

you are seated at the right hand of the Father:
    receive our prayer.

For you alone are the Holy One,
you alone are the Lord,
you alone are the Most High,
    Jesus Christ,
    with the Holy Spirit,
    in the glory of God the Father. Amen.

On other occasions the following is used

Lord, have mercy.		Kyrie eleison.
Christ, have mercy.	*or*	*Christe eleison.*
Lord, have mercy.		Kyrie eleison.

or this

Holy God,
Holy and Mighty,
Holy Immortal One,
Have mercy upon us.

The Collect of the Day

The Celebrant says to the people
        The Lord be with you.
People   And also with you.
Celebrant Let us pray.

The Celebrant says the Collect.

People   Amen.

The Lessons

The people sit. One or two Lessons, as appointed, are read, the Reader first saying
A Reading (Lesson) from _____ .

A citation giving chapter and verse may be added.

After each Reading, the Reader may say
        The Word of the Lord.
People   Thanks be to God.

or the Reader may say Here ends the Reading (Epistle).

Silence may follow.

A Psalm, hymn, or anthem may follow each Reading.

Then, all standing, the Deacon or a Priest reads the Gospel, first saying

The Holy Gospel of our Lord Jesus Christ according to _____ .

People   Glory to you, Lord Christ.

After the Gospel, the Reader says

The Gospel of the Lord.

People   Praise to you, Lord Christ.

The Sermon

On Sundays and other Major Feasts there follows, all standing

The Nicene Creed

We believe in one God,
   the Father, the Almighty,
   maker of heaven and earth,
   of all that is, seen and unseen.

We believe in one Lord, Jesus Christ,
   the only Son of God,
   eternally begotten of the Father,
   God from God, Light from Light,
   true God from true God,
   begotten, not made,
   of one Being with the Father.
   Through him all things were made.
   For us and for our salvation
     he came down from heaven:
by the power of the Holy Spirit
   he became incarnate from the Virgin Mary,
   and was made man.

For our sake he was crucified under Pontius Pilate;
    he suffered death and was buried.
      On the third day he rose again
        in accordance with the Scriptures;
    he ascended into heaven
      and is seated at the right hand of the Father.
He will come again in glory to judge the living and the dead,
    and his kingdom will have no end.

We believe in the Holy Spirit, the Lord, the giver of life,
    who proceeds from the Father and the Son.
    With the Father and the Son he is worshiped and glorified.
    He has spoken through the Prophets.
    We believe in one holy catholic and apostolic Church.
    We acknowledge one baptism for the forgiveness of sins.
    We look for the resurrection of the dead,
      and the life of the world to come. Amen.

The Prayers of the People

Prayer is offered with intercession for

The Universal Church, its members, and its mission
The Nation and all in authority
The welfare of the world
The concerns of the local community
Those who suffer and those in any trouble
The departed (with commemoration of a saint when appropriate)

Either of the following or some other form may be used.

Form A

The Leader and People pray responsively

In peace, we pray to you, Lord God.

Silence

For all people in their daily life and work;
For our families, friends, and neighbors, and for those who are alone.

For this community, the nation, and the world;
For all who work for justice, freedom, and peace.

For the just and proper use of your creation;
For the victims of hunger, fear, injustice, and oppression.

For all who are in danger, sorrow, or any kind of trouble;
For those who minister to the sick, the friendless, and the needy.

For the peace and unity of the Church of God;
For all who proclaim the Gospel, and all who seek the Truth.

For [*N.* our Presiding Bishop, and *N.* *(N.)* our Bishop(s); and for]
all bishops and other ministers;
For all who serve God in his Church.

For the special needs and concerns of this congregation.
Silence

The People may add their own petitions

Hear us, Lord;
For your mercy is great.

We thank you, Lord, for all the blessings of this life.
Silence

The People may add their own thanksgivings

We will exalt you, O God our King;
And praise your Name for ever and ever.

We pray for all who have died, that they may have a place in your
eternal kingdom.
Silence

The People may add their own petitions

Lord, let your loving-kindness be upon them;
Who put their trust in you.

The Celebrant concludes with this or some other Collect

Lord Jesus Christ, you said to your apostles, "Peace I give to you;
my own peace I leave with you;" Regard not our sins, but the
faith of your Church, and give to us the peace and unity of that
heavenly City, where with the Father and the Holy Spirit you live
and reign, now and for ever. *Amen.*

Form B

Leader

Let us pray for the holy Church of God in every place, and for all people in their needs.

For your Church throughout the world, that it may serve you in faith and unity, in the fellowship of the Holy Spirit, we pray to you, O Lord.
Lord, have mercy.

For all bishops, chaplains, and other ministers of Christ, we pray to you, O Lord.
Lord, have mercy.

That all nations may receive the Gospel of Christ, and serve you in peace, we pray to you, O Lord.
Lord, have mercy.

For the leaders of our country, especially *N.* our President [and for the leaders of our allies (especially *NN.*)], we pray to you, O Lord.
Lord, have mercy.

That all people may be delivered from oppression, hunger, fear, and injustice, we pray to you, O Lord.
Lord, have mercy.

For ourselves, our families, friends, and companions, we pray to you, O Lord.
Lord, have mercy.

For the sick, the wounded, the suffering, the bereaved, and all in special need (particularly *NN.*), we pray to you, O Lord.
Lord, have mercy.

For all who have died (especially *NN.*), we pray to you, O Lord.
Lord, have mercy.

Silence

The Celebrant concludes with this or some other Collect

Grant, O Lord, that we may serve you faithfully in this life, and finally enter with [_____ and] all your saints into the joy of your heavenly kingdom; through your Son Jesus Christ our Lord.
Amen.

If there is no celebration of the Communion, or if a priest is not available, the service concludes with the singing of a hymn (if desired), the Lord's Prayer, and with either the Grace or a blessing, or with the exchange of the Peace.

But if Communion is to be administered from the reserved Sacrament, the service continues on page 51.

Confession of Sin

A Confession of Sin is said here if it has not been said earlier. On occasion, the Confession may be omitted.

The Deacon or Celebrant says
Let us confess our sins against God and our neighbor.
Silence may be kept.

Minister and People
Most merciful God,
we confess that we have sinned against you
in thought, word, and deed,
by what we have done,
and by what we have left undone.
We have not loved you with our whole heart;
we have not loved our neighbors as ourselves.
We are truly sorry and we humbly repent.
For the sake of your Son Jesus Christ,
have mercy on us and forgive us;
that we may delight in your will,
and walk in your ways,
to the glory of your Name. Amen.

The Bishop when present, or the Priest, stands and says
Almighty God have mercy on you, forgive you all your sins through our Lord Jesus Christ, strengthen you in all goodness, and by the power of the Holy Spirit keep you in eternal life. *Amen.*

A deacon or lay person using the preceding form substitutes "us" for "you" and "our" for "your."

The Peace

All stand. The Celebrant says to the people

> The peace of the Lord be always with you.

People And also with you.

Then the Ministers and People may greet one another in the name of the Lord.

The Holy Communion

The Celebrant may begin the Offertory with a sentence of Scripture.

During the Offertory, a hymn, psalm, or anthem may be sung.

Representatives of the congregation bring the people's offerings of bread and wine, and money or other gifts, to the deacon or celebrant. The people stand while the offerings are presented and placed on the Altar.

The Great Thanksgiving

Eucharistic Prayer A

The people remain standing. The Celebrant, whether bishop or priest, faces them and sings or says

> The Lord be with you.

People And also with you.

Celebrant Lift up your hearts.

People We lift them to the Lord.

Celebrant Let us give thanks to the Lord our God.

People It is right to give him thanks and praise.

Then, facing the Holy Table, the Celebrant proceeds

It is right, and a good and joyful thing, always and everywhere to give thanks to you, Father Almighty, Creator of heaven and earth.

Here a Proper Preface is sung or said on all Sundays, and on other occasions as appointed.

Therefore we praise you, joining our voices with Angels and Archangels and with all the company of heaven, who for ever sing this hymn to proclaim the glory of your Name:

Celebrant and People

Holy, holy, holy Lord, God of power and might,
heaven and earth are full of your glory.
Hosanna in the highest.
Blessed is he who comes in the name of the Lord.
Hosanna in the highest.

The people stand or kneel.
Then the Celebrant continues

Holy and gracious Father: In your infinite love you made us for
yourself; and, when we had fallen into sin and become subject to
evil and death, you, in your mercy, sent Jesus Christ, your only and
eternal Son, to share our human nature, to live and die as one of us,
to reconcile us to you, the God and Father of all.

He stretched out his arms upon the cross, and offered himself, in
obedience to your will, a perfect sacrifice for the whole world.

*At the following words concerning the bread, the Celebrant is to hold it, or lay
a hand upon it; and at the words concerning the cup, to hold or place a hand
upon the cup and any other vessel containing wine to be consecrated.*

On the night he was handed over to suffering and death, our Lord
Jesus Christ took bread; and when he had given thanks to you, he
broke it, and gave it to his disciples, and said, "Take, eat: This is
my Body, which is given for you. Do this for the remembrance of
me."

After supper he took the cup of wine; and when he had given
thanks, he gave it to them, and said, "Drink this, all of you: This
is my Blood of the new Covenant, which is shed for you and for
many for the forgiveness of sins. Whenever you drink it, do this
for the remembrance of me."

Therefore we proclaim the mystery of faith:

Celebrant and People

Christ has died.
Christ is risen.
Christ will come again.

The Celebrant continues

We celebrate the memorial of our redemption, O Father, in this sacrifice of praise and thanksgiving. Recalling his death, resurrection, and ascension, we offer you these gifts.

Sanctify them by your Holy Spirit to be for your people the Body and Blood of your Son, the holy food and drink of new and unending life in him. Sanctify us also that we may faithfully receive this holy Sacrament, and serve you in unity, constancy, and peace; and at the last day bring us with all your saints into the joy of your eternal kingdom.

All this we ask through your Son Jesus Christ. By him, and with him, and in him, in the unity of the Holy Spirit all honor and glory is yours, Almighty Father, now and for ever. *AMEN.*

And now, as our Savior
Christ has taught us,
we are bold to say,

People and Celebrant

Our Father, who art in heaven,
  hallowed be thy Name,
  thy kingdom come,
  thy will be done,
    on earth as it is in heaven.
Give us this day our daily bread.
And forgive us our trespasses,
  as we forgive those
    who trepass against us.
And lead us not into temptation,
  but deliver us from evil.
For thine is the kingdom,
  and the power, and the glory,
  for ever and ever. Amen.

As our Savior Christ
has taught us,
we now pray,

Our Father in heaven,
  hallowed be your Name,
  your kingdom come,
  your will be done,
    on earth as in heaven.
Give us today our daily bread.
Forgive us our sins
  as we forgive those
    who sin against us.
Save us from the time of trial,
  and deliver us from evil.
For the kingdom, the power,
  and the glory are yours,
  now and for ever. Amen.

The Breaking of the Bread

The Celebrant breaks the consecrated Bread.

A period of silence is kept.

Then may be sung or said

[Alleluia.] Christ our Passover is sacrificed for us;
Therefore let us keep the feast. [*Alleluia.*]

In Lent, Alleluia is omitted, and may be omitted at other times except during Easter Season.

In place of, or in addition to, the preceding, some other suitable anthem may be used.

Facing the people, the Celebrant says the following Invitation

The Gifts of God for the People of God.

and may add Take them in remembrance that Christ died for you, and feed on him in your hearts by faith, with thanksgiving.

The ministers receive the Sacrament in both kinds, and then immediately deliver it to the people.

The Bread and the Cup are given to the communicants with these words

The Body (Blood) of our Lord Jesus Christ keep you in everlasting life. [*Amen.*]

or with these words

The Body of Christ, the bread of heaven. [*Amen.*]
The Blood of Christ, the cup of salvation.[*Amen.*]

During the ministration of Communion, hymns, psalms, or anthems may be sung.

When necessary, the Celebrant consecrates additional bread and wine, using the form on page 49.

After Communion, the Celebrant says

Let us pray.

Celebrant and People

Eternal God, heavenly Father,
you have graciously accepted us as living members
of your Son our Savior Jesus Christ,
and you have fed us with spiritual food
in the Sacrament of his Body and Blood.
Send us now into the world in peace,
and grant us strength and courage
to love and serve you
with gladness and singleness of heart;
through Christ our Lord. Amen.

or the following

Almighty and everliving God,
we thank you for feeding us with the spiritual food
of the most precious Body and Blood
of your Son our Savior Jesus Christ;
and for assuring us in these holy mysteries
that we are living members of the Body of your Son,
and heirs of your eternal kingdom.
And now, Father, send us out
to do the work you have given us to do,
to love and serve you
as faithful witnesses of Christ our Lord.
To him, to you, and to the Holy Spirit,
be honor and glory, now and for ever. Amen.

The Bishop when present, or the Priest, may bless the people.

The Deacon, or the Celebrant, dismisses them with these words

	Let us go forth in the name of Christ.
People	Thanks be to God.
or this	
Deacon	Go in peace to love and serve the Lord.
People	Thanks be to God.
or this	
Deacon	Let us go forth into the world, rejoicing in the power of the Spirit.
People	Thanks be to God.
or this	
Deacon	Let us bless the Lord.
People	Thanks be to God.

From the Easter Vigil through the Day of Pentecost "Alleluia, alleluia" may be added to any of the dismissals.

The People respond

Thanks be to God. Alleluia, alleluia.

ADDITIONAL DIRECTIONS

The Collects, Psalms, and Lessons used at celebrations of the Holy Eucharist are ordinarily those appointed in the Book of Common Prayer. When the situation warrants, however, other Propers may be used, or a selection may be made from material included in this book.

When it is necessary to shorten the service, the form provided on page 50 is used.

Lay persons appointed by the chaplain should normally be assigned the reading of the lessons which precede the Gospel, and may lead the Prayers of the People.

Lay persons specifically licensed by the Bishop for the Armed Forces may administer the chalice when invited to do so by the celebrant.

In the absence of a priest, a licensed lay reader may lead the first part of this service, concluding it as described at the top of page 43.

Appropriate parts of the service may be sung as desired. The texts of anthems are to be from Holy Scripture, or from the Book of Common Prayer, or from texts congruent with them. Hymns may be selected from *The Hymnal 1982*, from the *Book of Worship for United States Forces*, or from this book.

FORM FOR CONSECRATING ADDITIONAL ELEMENTS

Hear us, O heavenly Father, and with your Word and Holy Spirit bless and sanctify this bread (wine) that it, also, may be the Sacrament of the precious Body (Blood) of your Son Jesus Christ our Lord, who took bread (the cup) and said, "This is my Body (Blood)." *Amen.*

THE HOLY EUCHARIST: A SHORTER FORM

This form is intended to enable military chaplains of the Episcopal Church to celebrate the Eucharist under conditions which make it not feasible to use the full form given in the Book of Common Prayer and on pages 37-48 of this book.

1. A passage from the Gospel, appropriate to the day or occasion, is read.

2. After the Reading, the chaplain may comment on it briefly.

3. Suitable prayers may be offered. One of the forms of the Prayers of the People on pages 40-42 may be used.

4. The Confession of Sin, page 43, may be said.

5. The service continues with the Peace and Offertory, page 44.

In place of the usual postcommunion prayer, the chaplain may use the following:

Gracious Father, we give you praise and thanks for this Holy Communion of the Body and Blood of your beloved Son Jesus Christ, the pledge of our redemption; and we pray that it may bring us forgiveness of our sins, strength in our weakness, and everlasting salvation; through Jesus Christ our Lord. *Amen.*

In cases of necessity, the chaplain may begin with the Offertory, but it is desirable that a brief passage from the Gospel (such as Reading no. 20, page 107) be read first.

COMMUNION FROM
THE RESERVED SACRAMENT

This form is intended for use by military chaplains of the Episcopal Church in administering the already consecrated Sacrament to individuals who, for reasonable cause, cannot be present at a public celebration of the Eucharist.

It is also intended for use by duly authorized and licensed lay eucharistic ministers in administering Communion to congregations and individuals where there is no chaplain.

When used with individuals, the service begins with a passage of Scripture appropriate to the day or occasion. A brief comment on the Reading may follow, and suitable prayers may be offered.

When used with a congregation, the service begins with the Liturgy of the Word of God, page 37, as far as the end of the Prayers of the People.

The service then continues as follows:

Confession of Sin

A Confession of Sin may be said.

The Minister says

Let us confess our sins against God and our neighbor.

Silence may be kept.

Minister and People

Most merciful God,
we confess that we have sinned against you
in thought, word, and deed,
by what we have done,
and by what we have left undone.
We have not loved you with our whole heart;
we have not loved our neighbors as ourselves.
We are truly sorry and we humbly repent.
For the sake of your Son Jesus Christ,
have mercy on us and forgive us;
that we may delight in your will,
and walk in your ways,
to the glory of your Name. Amen.

The Chaplain then says

Almighty God have mercy upon you, forgive you all your sins
through our Lord Jesus Christ, strengthen you in all goodness,
and by the power of the Holy Spirit keep you in eternal life.
Amen.

*A lay eucharistic minister using the preceding form substitutes "us" for "you"
and "our" for "your."*

The Peace

The Peace is then exchanged

Minister   The peace of the Lord be always with you.
People   And also with you.

The Communion

The Lord's Prayer is said, the Minister first saying

Let us pray in the words our Savior Christ has taught us.

Our Father, who art in heaven,
  hallowed be thy Name,
  thy kingdom come,
  thy will be done,
    on earth as it is in heaven.
Give us this day our daily bread.
And forgive us our trespasses,
  as we forgive those
    who trespass against us.
And lead us not into temptation,
  but deliver us from evil.
For thine is the kingdom,
  and the power, and the glory,
  for ever and ever. Amen.

Our Father in heaven,
  hallowed be your Name,
  your kingdom come,
  your will be done,
    on earth as in heaven.
Give us today our daily bread.
Forgive us our sins
  as we forgive those
    who sin against us.
Save us from the time of trial
  and deliver us from evil.
For the kingdom, the power,
  and the glory are yours,
  now and for ever. Amen.

The Minister may say the following Invitation

The Gifts of God for the People of God.
and may add Take them in remembrance that Christ died for you,
and feed on him in your hearts by faith, with thanksgiving.

The Sacrament is administered with the following words

The Body (Blood) of our Lord Jesus Christ keep you in everlasting life. [*Amen.*]

or with these words

The Body of Christ, the bread of heaven. [*Amen.*]
The Blood of Christ, the cup of salvation. [*Amen.*]

or, in Spanish:

El Cuerpo (la Sangre) de nuestro Señor Jesucristo te guarde en la vida eterna. [*Amén.*]

o con estas:

El Cuerpo de Cristo, pan del cielo. [*Amén.*]
La Sangre de Cristo, cáliz de salvación. [*Amén.*]

After Communion, the Lay Eucharistic Minister and People say one of the postcommunion prayers on pages 47-48, after which the Minister dismisses the people.

When this form is used with individuals, however, the following postcommunion prayer may be used instead

Gracious Father, we give you praise and thanks for this Holy Communion of the Body and Blood of your beloved Son Jesus Christ, the pledge of our redemption; and we pray that it may bring us forgiveness of our sins, strength in our weakness, and everlasting salvation; through Jesus Christ our Lord. *Amen.*

The service then concludes with a blessing by the chaplain or with this dismissal

Let us bless the Lord.
Thanks be to God.

WHEN HOLY COMMUNION
IS NOT AVAILABLE

Wherever they may be, members of the Church should always try to receive Holy Communion regularly. It is the most sacred means which Christ has given us to unite us to himself and to his Church. If you are stationed where there is no Episcopal chaplain, it may be possible for you to attend a nearby civilian parish church. In many overseas areas, you may receive the sacraments from clergy of other Anglican Churches. These Churches have the same faith as the Episcopal Church, their services are very similar to ours, and you may look to them as to your own Church. The Episcopal Church is also in communion with several other Churches in Europe and Asia. There are also some Lutheran Churches in which you will be welcomed, both overseas and in North America.

It may well happen, however, that you are stationed in a place where none of these opportunities is open to you. You may, and indeed should, attend some Christian service of worship each week. Yet you will miss receiving Holy Communion in the way that is familiar to you. Men and women in the service wonder whether they may receive Communion in some other Church. Many chaplains of various Christian bodies will be willing to administer to you. Whether or not you wish to receive their ministrations will depend on several factors.

It is not generally recommended that you receive any sacramental rites in another Church (a) unless the priest or minister of that Church is willing for you to do so, (b) unless you are actually cut off from the ministrations of your own Church for a long period, (c) unless the faith of the other denomination is based on Holy Scripture and the Creeds, and its practice of the sacraments is comparable to your own, and (d) unless you can participate in its worship in an honest and prayerful manner without compromising your own faith and Church loyalty.

If you are attending the Lord's Supper or Mass in another Church, and are not going to communicate, it is recommended that while others are receiving Communion, you remain in silent prayer. The prayer "For Communion with Christ," given on the next page may be useful to you at such times.

WHEN YOU CANNOT ATTEND WORSHIP

On Sundays, if you cannot attend a service of worship, it is suggested that you perform the following devotions privately.

1. Read the Lessons and Psalm for the Day appointed in the Book of Common Prayer, or one or more of the Bible Readings and Psalms given in this book, See pages 99 and 73 for suggestions.

2. Say the Apostles' Creed (unless you have already said it in your morning prayers).

3. Say one of the forms of the Prayers of the People (pages 40-42) and, if desired, the Confession of Sin (page 43).

4. Then say this prayer:

A Prayer for Communion with Christ

In union, O Lord, with your faithful people at every altar of your Church, where the Holy Eucharist is now being celebrated, I desire to offer to you praise and thanksgiving. I remember your death, Lord Christ; I proclaim your resurrection; I await your coming in glory. And since I cannot receive you today in the Sacrament of your Body and Blood, I beseech you to come spiritually into my heart. Cleanse and strengthen me with your grace, Lord Jesus, and let me never be separated from you. May I live in you, and you in me, in this life and in the life to come. Amen.

The General Thanksgiving (page 126) may also be used.

5. Conclude your devotions with these words:

To Christ our Lord who loves us, and washed us in his own blood, and made us a kingdom of priests to serve his God and Father, to him be glory and dominion for ever and ever. Amen.

CONFIRMATION

When possible, Confirmation, Reception, and the Reaffirmation
of Baptismal Vows take place at a service of Holy Baptism.
If there are to be no baptisms when the bishop comes for
Confirmation, the following order is used.

1. *The service begins as appointed for Holy Baptism (page 25).*

2. *After the Sermon, the Bishop says*

   The Candidate(s) will now be presented.

   Presenters I present *these persons* for Confirmation.

   or I present *these persons* to be received into this
   Communion.

   or I present *these persons* who *desire* to reaffirm *their*
   baptismal vows.

   The Bishop asks the candidates

   Do you reaffirm your renunciation of evil?

   Candidate I do.

   Bishop Do you renew your commitment to Jesus Christ?

   Candidate I do, and with God's grace I will follow him as my
   Savior and Lord.

*After all have been presented, the Bishop addresses the congregation,
saying*

Will you who witness these vows do all in your power to support
these persons in *their* life in Christ?

   People We will.

   The Bishop then says these or similar words

   Let us join with *those* who *are* committing *themselves* to Christ
   and renew our own baptismal covenant.

3. *The Baptismal Covenant, pages 28-29, then follows (as far as the
   Prayers for the Candidates).*

4. *The service continues with "At Confirmation, Reception, or Reaffirmation" on page 32.*

DECÁLOGO

1. Yo soy el Señor tu Dios que te sacó de la servidumbre. No tendrás otros dioses delante de mí.

2. No te harás imagen alguna.

3. No invocarás en falso el Nombre del Señor tu Dios.

4. Recuerda el día del sábado para santificarlo.

5. Honra a tu padre y a tu madre.

6. No asesinarás.

7. No cometerás adulterio.

8. No robarás.

9. No darás testimonio falso.

10. No codiciarás nada de lo que pertenezca a tu prójimo.

Exodo 20; Deuteronomio 5

SUMARIO DE LA LEY

Jesús dijo: "El primer mandamiento es éste: Escucha, Israel: El Señor nuestro Dios es el único Señor. Amarás al Señor tu Dios con todo tu corazón, con toda tu alma, con toda tu mente y con todas tus fuerzas. El segundo es éste: Amarás a tu prójimo como a ti mismo. No hay otro mandamiento mayor que éstos".

San Marcos 12:29-31

THE TEN COMMANDMENTS

1. I am the Lord your God who brought you out of bondage.
   You shall have no other gods but me.

2. You shall not make for yourself any idol.

3. You shall not invoke with malice the Name of the Lord
   your God.

4. Remember the Sabbath Day and keep it holy.

5. Honor your father and your mother.

6. You shall not commit murder.

7. You shall not commit adultery.

8. You shall not steal.

9. You shall not be a false witness.

10. You shall not covet anything that belongs to your neighbor.

Exodus 20; Deuteronomy 5.

THE SUMMARY OF THE LAW

Jesus said, "The first commandment is this: Hear, O Israel: The
Lord our God is the only Lord. Love the Lord your God with all
your heart, with all your soul, with all your mind, and with all
your strength. The second is this: Love your neighbor as yourself. There is no other commandment greater than these."

Mark 12:29-31

ABOUT PENITENCE AND RECONCILIATION

REPENTANCE AND FORGIVENESS

All of us fall into sin at one time or another. Our sins may appear very small, or very large, but in either case they grieve God, they directly or indirectly harm others, and they reduce our own integrity and spiritual strength. To ignore or disregard the fact of sin is unrealistic, because sin causes great harm both to individuals and to society. On the other hand, to think about our sins continually can lead to depression, and sometimes to further wrongdoing.

God through Christ has given us the remedy for sin. This remedy is *penitence* or *repentance*. By regular penitence a Christian can increasingly overcome his or her sins, shortcomings, and weaknesses; one can become more pleasing to God and to one's neighbors. Penitence has several stages. First, there is *self-examination*, the process of looking back and seeing which of our thoughts, words, and actions have been sinful. Second, there is *confession*, in which we admit our sins and honestly accept the guilt of having done wrong. In confession we go on to ask God to forgive us. Third, there is *reparation*, or willingness to restore and make good our relation to others, and to forgive those who have sinned against us. *God promises forgiveness to those who truly repent.*

The New Testament (1 Corinthians 11:28) teaches us that before coming to Communion we should examine our lives and conduct, and the Book of Common Prayer re-echoes this warning (pages 316-317). Our private self-examination and prayer for forgiveness prepares us to participate in the general Confession of Sin frequently used at the Eucharist and to receive Absolution (the priest's declaration of forgiveness). We need not wait until Sunday morning to examine our consciences, however. The faithful Christian will find it best to make a brief self-examination every evening, and to pray for God's forgiveness of the sins and shortcomings of the past day.

CONFESSION TO A PRIEST

Unfortunately, we sometimes fall into more serious sin, and our consciences continue to bother us. It is for this reason that the Book of Common Prayer provides that we may confess our sins privately, in the presence of a priest. By doing this, we receive the benefit of the priest's counsel and spiritual guidance, as well as individual assurance of God's pardon and absolution.

Those who desire to make their confession in this way, but have never done so before, should consult with the priest beforehand for guidance. Such a confession is a most solemn act, and is performed in a place of privacy. The priest is strictly bound to treat all that is said in complete confidence.

CONFESSION TO A LAY PERSON

When necessary, such as when someone is badly wounded or dying, or is in serious depression, and there is no priest available, a lay person may hear the confession of another Christian. A lay person who does this is bound by the same rule of complete confidence, and must never, under any circumstances, reveal anything that has been said in the confession. The form given below is used, but in place of the Absolution (which a lay person may not pronounce), the Declaration of Forgiveness given at the end of the form is used.

THE RECONCILIATION OF A PENITENT

The Penitent begins

Bless me, for I have sinned.

The Priest says

The Lord be in your heart and upon your lips that you may truly and humbly confess your sins: In the Name of the Father, and of the Son, and of the Holy Spirit. *Amen.*

Penitent

I confess to Almighty God, to his Church, and to you, that I have
sinned by my own fault in thought, word, and deed, in things
done and left undone; especially _____. For these
and all other sins which I cannot now remember, I am truly sorry.
I pray God to have mercy on me. I firmly intend amendment of
life, and I humbly beg forgiveness of God and his Church, and
ask you for counsel, direction, and absolution.

Here the Priest may offer counsel, direction, and comfort.

The Priest then pronounces this absolution

Our Lord Jesus Christ, who has left power to his Church to absolve all sinners who truly repent and believe in him, of his great
mercy forgive you all your offenses; and by his authority committed to me, I absolve you from all your sins: In the Name of the
Father, and of the Son, and of the Holy Spirit. *Amen.*

or this

Our Lord Jesus Christ, who offered himself to be sacrificed for us
to the Father, and who conferred power on his Church to forgive
sins, absolve you through my ministry by the grace of the Holy
Spirit, and restore you in the perfect peace of the Church. *Amen.*

The Priest adds

The Lord has put away all your sins.

Penitent   Thanks be to God.

The Priest concludes

Go (*or* abide) in peace, and pray for me, a sinner.

DECLARATION OF FORGIVENESS
TO BE USED BY A DEACON OR LAY PERSON

Our Lord Jesus Christ, who offered himself to be sacrificed for us
to the Father, forgives your sins by the grace of the Holy Spirit.
Amen.

MINISTRATION TO THE SICK OR WOUNDED

It is natural to turn to God in prayer when suffering from sickness or wounds. Such times can be opportunities for spiritual growth. God can help us learn to endure the pain, annoyance, loneliness, and boredom which come to us. A number of the Psalms, Bible Readings, and prayers in this book are appropriate for use at such times. See pages 73 and 99 for Psalms and Readings, and pages 122-124 for prayers. These may be used by the person alone, or by a chaplain or lay reader visiting the sick.

If you are sick or wounded, and your conscience is bothering you, you should speak to the chaplain. If you wish to confess your sins privately, the form on page 60-61 will be used. Otherwise, the chaplain will lead you in saying the general Confession of Sin on page 43 and give you absolution.

Then, if you desire it, the chaplain will perform the Church's special ministry of healing by laying hands on you (and anointing you with oil), using the following form:

Laying on of Hands and Anointing

If oil for the Anointing of the Sick is to be blessed, the Priest says

O Lord, holy Father, giver of health and salvation: Send your Holy Spirit to sanctify this oil; that, as your holy apostles anointed many that were sick and healed them, so may those who in faith and repentance receive this holy unction be made whole; through Jesus Christ our Lord, who lives and reigns with you and the Holy Spirit, one God, for ever and ever. *Amen.*

The following anthem is said

Savior of the world, by your cross and precious blood you have redeemed us;
Save us, and help us, we humbly beseech you, O Lord.

The Priest then lays hands upon the sick person, and says one of the following

N., I lay my hands upon you in the Name of the Father, and of the Son, and of the Holy Spirit, beseeching our Lord Jesus Christ to sustain you with his presence, to drive away all sickness of body and spirit, and to give you that victory of life and peace which will enable you to serve him both now and evermore. *Amen.*

or this

N., I lay my hands upon you in the Name of our Lord and Savior Jesus Christ, beseeching him to uphold you and fill you with his grace, that you may know the healing power of his love. *Amen.*

If the person is to be anointed, the Priest dips a thumb in the holy oil, and makes the sign of the cross on the sick person's forehead (or elsewhere when necessary), saying

N., I anoint you with oil in the Name of the Father, and of the Son, and of the Holy Spirit. *Amen.*

The Priest may add

As you are outwardly anointed with this holy oil, so may our heavenly Father grant you the inward anointing of the Holy Spirit. Of his great mercy, may he forgive you your sins, release you from suffering, and restore you to wholeness and strength. May he deliver you from all evil, preserve you in all goodness, and bring you to everlasting life; through Jesus Christ our Lord. *Amen.*

In cases of necessity, a deacon or lay person may perform the anointing, using oil blessed by a bishop or priest.

If Communion is not to follow, the Lord's Prayer is now said.

The Priest concludes

The Almighty Lord, who is a strong tower to all who put their trust in him, to whom all things in heaven, on earth, and under the earth bow and obey: Be now and evermore your defense, and make you know and feel that the only Name under heaven given for health and salvation is the Name of our Lord Jesus Christ. *Amen.*

Holy Communion

In administering Holy Communion to the sick or wounded, the chaplain may either (1) celebrate the Eucharist, using the form on page 50, or (2) give Communion from the reserved Sacrament, using the form on page 51. In either case, if the laying on of hands (and anointing) has immediately preceded, the chaplain begins the Communion rite with the Peace.

FOR THE DYING

When Facing Death Yourself

If you are about to die, say the Lord's Prayer and the Apostles' Creed. In your own words, ask God to forgive the sins you have committed, to have mercy on all persons you have wronged or injured, and to forgive all who have sinned against you. Pray for your family and any others who especially deserve your prayers. Sum up your prayers with words such as these:

Almighty God, I entrust all who are dear to me to your never-failing care and love, for this life and the life to come; knowing that you are doing for them better things than I can desire or pray for; through Jesus Christ our Lord. Amen.

As your earthly life comes to a close, use these words which Christ used:

Father, into your hands I commend my spirit.

Cuando en Peligro de Muerte

Si usted está a punto de morir, diga el Padre Nuestro y el Credo de los Após- toles. Usando sus propias palabras, pida perdón a Dios por todos sus pecados, que tenga misericordia sobre todos aquéllos que usted ha engañado o herido y que perdone a todos aquéllos que han pecado contra usted. Ore por su familia y por todos aquéllos que especialmente merecen sus oraciones. Resuma sus ora- ciones con frases como la siguiente:

Omnipotente Dios, encomiendo a aquéllos que me son queridos a tu fiel cuidado y amor, en esta vida y la venidera; sabiendo que estás haciendo por ellos mejores cosas que las que pueda desear o suplicar; por Jesucristo nuestro Señor. Amén.

Al llegar tu vida al final, usa esta palabras que Cristo dijo:

Padre, en tus manos encomiendo mi espíritu.

Commendation of the Dying

If you are with someone who is dying, say the Lord's Prayer. If possible, have the person say it with you. If the person cannot speak, say the prayer for him or her. (People who are dying can often hear even if they seem unconscious.) You may also say the Creed (inside front cover).

If the person is not baptized, and desires to be, use the form for Emergency Baptism on page 34 or 35.

If there is time, you may read a suitable Psalm, such as Psalm 23 (page 75, 76, or 93), or a Bible Reading, such as no. 38 (page 113).

The Litany at the Time of Death, page 68, may also be said.

At the moment of death, this commendation is said over a dying Christian:

Depart, O Christian soul, out of this world;
In the Name of God the Father Almighty who created you;
In the Name of Jesus Christ who redeemed you;
In the Name of the Holy Spirit who sanctifies you.
May your rest be this day in peace,
   and your dwelling place in the Paradise of God.

When the person has died, say this commendatory prayer:

Into your hands, O merciful Savior, we commend your servant *N*.
Acknowledge, we humbly beseech you, a sheep of your own fold,
a lamb of your own flock, a sinner of your own redeeming.
Receive *him* into the arms of your mercy, into the blessed rest of
everlasting peace, and into the glorious company of the saints in
light. *Amen.*

May *his* soul and the souls of all the departed, through the mercy
of God, rest in peace. *Amen.*

The following commendation may be used for one who does not profess the Christian faith:

Almighty God, creator of us all, and lover of the human race: We
commend our brother (sister) *N.* into your merciful hands.
Deliver *him* from all fear, strengthen *him* with your presence, and
give *him* peace; through Jesus Christ our Lord. *Amen.*

ACT OF CONTRITION AND COMMENDATION OF THE DYING (ROMAN CATHOLIC)

If the person who is dying is a Roman Catholic, remind him or her to make an Act of Perfect Contrition, using one of the following or similar words. If necessary, say the words yourself and have the person say them after you.

O my God, I am sorry for my sins because I have offended you. I know I should love you above all things. Forgive me my sins. Help me to do penance, to do better, and to avoid anything that might lead me to sin. Amen.

or this

Jesus, I love you and am sorry for having offended you. Amen.

If the person cannot speak, or appears to be unconscious or dead, speak directly into the person's ear. Tell him or her that you will recite an Act of Contrition, and to try to make this prayer with you, either in words or in their heart. Then say the shorter form given above.

If there is time, you may read a suitable Psalm, such as Psalm 23 (page 75, 76, or 93), or a Bible Reading, such as no. 38 (page 113).

At the moment of death, say this commendation:

In the name of God the Father Almighty who created you,
in the name of Jesus Christ, Son of the living God,
   who suffered for you,
in the name of the Holy Spirit, who was poured out
   upon you,
go forth, faithful Christian.
May you live in peace this day,
may your home be with God in Zion,
with Mary the virgin Mother of God,
with Joseph, and all the angels and saints.

CONFESSION FOR THE CRITICALLY ILL
(JEWISH)

Lord My God and God of my ancestors I acknowledge that in Your hand alone is my recovery or my death. May it be Your will that I be completely healed. Yet if it be Your will that I die, then I shall accept my death lovingly at Your hands. May my death be my atonement for all my sins, transgressions, and wrongs that I have done before You. May I receive a portion of that goodness that is stored up for the righteous. Make me to know the path of life, the fullness of blissful joy in Your Presence at Your right hand forevermore.

O You who are the Father of the fatherless and the guardian of the widow, protect my beloved family, whose souls are linked to mine. Into Your hand I commend my spirit; You have redeemed me, O God of truth. Amen and Amen.

When the end is approaching:

The Lord is King; the Lord was King; the Lord shall reign forever and ever. *(Said three times.)*

Blessed is His glorious kingdom forever and ever. *(Said three times.)*

The Lord, He is God. *(Said seven times.)*

Hear, O Israel: the Lord is our God; the Lord is One!

She-ma Yis-ra-eil: A-do-nai E-lo-hei-nu; A-do-nai e-chad!

LITANY AT THE TIME OF DEATH

This Litany may be said by one or more persons when someone is dying, or shortly afterwards. It may also be used at funeral or memorial services.

God the Father,
Have mercy on your servant.

God the Son,
Have mercy on your servant.

God the Holy Spirit,
Have mercy on your servant.

Holy Trinity, one God,
Have mercy on your servant.

From all evil, from all sin, from all tribulation,
Good Lord, deliver him.

By your holy Incarnation, by your Cross and Passion, by your precious Death and Burial,
Good Lord, deliver him.

By your glorious Resurrection and Ascension, and by the Coming of the Holy Spirit,
Good Lord, deliver him.

We sinners beseech you to hear us, Lord Christ: That it may please you to deliver the soul of your servant from the power of evil, and from eternal death,
We beseech you to hear us, good Lord.

That it may please you mercifully to pardon all *his* sins.
We beseech you to hear us, good Lord.

That it may please you to grant *him* a place of refreshment and everlasting blessedness,
We beseech you to hear us, good Lord.

That it may please you to give *him* joy and gladness in your kingdom, with your saints in light,
We beseech you to hear us, good Lord.

Jesus, Lamb of God:
Have mercy on him.

Jesus, bearer of our sins:
Have mercy on him.

Jesus, redeemer of the world:
Give him *your peace.*

Lord, have mercy.
Christ, have mercy.
Lord, have mercy.

Officiant and People

Our Father, who art in heaven,
hallowed be thy Name,
thy kingdom come,
thy will be done,
on earth as it is in heaven.
Give us this day our daily bread.
And forgive us our trespasses,
as we forgive those
who trespass against us.
And lead us not into temptation,
but deliver us from evil.

Our Father in heaven,
hallowed be your Name,
your kingdom come,
your will be done,
on earth as in heaven.
Give us today our daily bread.
Forgive us our sins
as we forgive those
who sin against us.
Save us from the time of trial,
and deliver us from evil.

The Leader then says this Collect

Let us pray.

Deliver your servant, *N.*, O Sovereign Lord Christ, from all evil,
and set *him* free from every bond; that *he* may rest with all your
saints in the eternal habitations; where with the Father and the
Holy Spirit you live and reign, one God, for ever and ever. *Amen.*

*If the person is at the point of death, continue with the Commendation on
page 65.*

*If the person has already died, continue with the Commendatory Prayer
"Into your hands" on page 65.*

BURIAL OF THE DEAD AND MEMORIAL SERVICES

Funeral Services and Memorial Services are ordinarily conducted by a chaplain. When the person who has died was a communicant of the Church, it is appropriate that the Episcopal chaplain celebrate the Eucharist at such services.

In the absence of a chaplain, a lay reader or other member of the Church may lead the service, using the form for "A Service of Worship" on page 22. Prayer no. 32, page 124, is appropriate for an opening prayer. For suggested Readings and Psalms, see pages 99 and 73. For the Prayers of the People, the Litany at the Time of Death may be used, or the leader may choose other prayers.

A licensed lay reader may also use the form on page 491 of the Book of Common Prayer.

Emergency Burial on Land or at Sea

Put some earth on the body, or cast the body reverently into the sea, and say these or similar words

In sure and certain hope of the resurrection to eternal life through our Lord Jesus Christ, we commend to Almighty God our brother (sister) *N.*, and we commit *his* body to the ground (*or* to the deep); earth to earth, ashes to ashes, dust to dust. The Lord bless *him* and keep *him*, the Lord make his face to shine upon *him* and be gracious to *him*, the Lord lift up his countenance upon *him* and give *him* peace. *Amen.*

Then say these prayers

Our Father . . .

Rest eternal grant to *him*, O Lord;
And let light perpetual shine upon him.

May *his* soul, and the souls of all the departed, through the mercy of God, rest in peace. *Amen.*

Psalms and Canticles

PSALMS AND CANTICLES

The Psalms are the prayers and hymns of the Hebrew people, and the part of the Bible especially intended for use in public or private worship. Canticles are ancient hymns of the Christian Church, or songs taken from other parts of the Bible. They are given here in the translation used in the Book of Common Prayer of the Episcopal Church. Other Churches use different translations of the Psalms and Canticles, but the meaning is the same.

Because they were used by Jesus himself, Christians interpret many of the Psalms in a special way. For example, because Christ spoke the opening words of Psalm 22 while dying on the cross, Christians understand the whole Psalm as a prayer of Jesus. Similarly, Christians interpret many of the references to "Israel," "Zion," and "Jerusalem" as applying also to the Christian Church.

When Psalms are used in private meditation, it is helpful to stop after each Psalm and offer a brief prayer—in one's own words—about something the Psalm has brought to mind.

A table of suggested Psalms for morning and evening is on page 7.

The asterisks (*) at the ends of lines show where the chant changes when the Psalms are sung. When they are read, a distinct pause should be made at each asterisk.

The following doxology may be said after the Psalms appointed for morning and evening

Glory to the Father, and to the Son,
   and to the Holy Spirit:*
as it was in the beginning, is now,
   and will be for ever. Amen.

For Psalms in Spanish, see pages 93-96.

A GUIDE TO THE PSALMS

FOR THE CHURCH YEAR

Advent 24, 63, 67, 85, 146
Christmas 85, 98, 150
Epiphany 67, 100, 146
Sundays after Epiphany 23, 46, 63, 84, 95, 121, 122
Lent 1, 22, 51, 103, 130
Easter Season 114, 118, 146, 150
Ascension Day 24, 98, 150
The Day of Pentecost 46, 122, 139
Trinity Sunday 100, 146, 150
Other Sundays after Pentecost *Any Psalm may be chosen*
Saint's Days and Other Feasts 46, 63, 67, 95, 98, 103, 146, 150
Thanksgiving Day 65, 67, 100
Other National Days 67, 98, 100, 146

FOR PARTICULAR NEEDS

God the Creator 65, 95, 100, 146
God the Redeemer 103, 114, 118, 130
God the Holy Spirit 51, 139
Baptism or Confirmation 23, 84, 122, 139
Burial and Memorial Services 23, 46, 121, 130, 139
The Church 46, 84, 122
God's Law 1, 146
God's Protection 23, 46, 121, 139
Holy Communion 23, 63, 84, 122
Meditations 103, 139
Praise 67, 95, 98, 100, 103, 146, 150
Prayer for Help 121, 130
Prayer for Reassurance 23, 46, 139
Repentance 51, 130
Sickness 23, 51, 121, 130, 139
Thanksgiving for Deliverance 103, 146

Psalm 1. The two ways

Happy are they who have not walked in the counsel of
                            the wicked,*
   nor lingered in the way of sinners,
   nor sat in the seats of the scornful!
Their delight is in the law of the LORD,*
   and they meditate on his law day and night.
They are like trees planted by streams of water,
bearing fruit in due season, with leaves that do not wither,*
   everything they do shall prosper.
It is not so with the wicked;*
   they are like chaff which the wind blows away.
Therefore the wicked shall not stand upright when
                            judgment comes,*
   nor the sinner in the council of the righteous.
For the LORD knows the way of the righteous,*
   but the way of the wicked is doomed.

Psalm 22:1-11, 14-18. Jesus' prayer from the cross

My God, my God, why have you forsaken me?*
   and are so far from my cry
   and from the words of my distress?
O my God, I cry in the daytime, but you do not answer,*
   by night as well, but I find no rest.
Yet you are the Holy One,*
   enthroned upon the praises of Israel.
Our forefathers put their trust in you;*
   they trusted, and you delivered them.
They cried out to you and were delivered;*
   they trusted in you and were not put to shame.
But as for me, I am a worm and no man,*
   scorned by all and despised by the people.
All who see me laugh me to scorn;*
   they curl their lips and wag their heads, saying,
"He trusted in the LORD; let him deliver him;*
   let him rescue him, if he delights in him."

Yet you are he who took me out of the womb,*
  and kept me safe upon my mother's breast.
I have been entrusted to you ever since I was born;*
  you were my God when I was still in my mother's womb.
Be not far from me, for trouble is near,*
  and there is none to help.
I am poured out like water;
all my bones are out of joint;*
  my heart within my breast is melting wax.
My mouth is dried out like a pot-sherd;
my tongue sticks to the roof of my mouth;*
  and you have laid me in the dust of the grave.
Packs of dogs close me in,
and gangs of evildoers circle around me;*
  they pierce my hands and my feet;
  I can count all my bones.
They stare and gloat over me;*
  they divide my garments among them;
  they cast lots for my clothing.
Be not far away, O Lord;*
  you are my strength; hasten to help me.

Psalm 23. The good shepherd

The Lord is my shepherd;*
  I shall not be in want.
He makes me lie down in green pastures*
  and leads me beside still waters.
He revives my soul*
  and guides me along right pathways for his Name's sake.
Though I walk through the valley of the shadow of death,
I shall fear no evil;*
  for you are with me;
  your rod and your staff, they comfort me.
You spread a table before me in the presence of those
                          who trouble me;*
  you have anointed my head with oil,
  and my cup is running over.

Surely your goodness and mercy shall follow me all the days
of my life,*
   and I will dwell in the house of the LORD for ever.

Psalm 23.   King James Version

The LORD is my shepherd;*
   I shall not want.
He maketh me to lie down in green pastures;*
   he leadeth me beside still waters.
He restoreth my soul;*
   he leadeth me in the paths of righteousness
   for his Name's sake.
Yea, though I walk through the valley of the shadow of death,
I will fear no evil;*
   for thou art with me;
   thy rod and thy staff, they comfort me.
Thou preparest a table before me
in the presence of mine enemies;*
   thou anointest my head with oil;
   my cup runneth over.
Surely thy goodness and mercy shall follow me
all the days of my life,*
   and I will dwell in the house of the LORD for ever.

Psalm 24.   The Lord enters his holy place

The earth is the LORD's and all that is in it,*
   the world and all who dwell therein.
For it is he who founded it upon the seas*
   and made it firm upon the rivers of the deep.
"Who can ascend the hill of the LORD?*
   and who can stand in his holy place?"
"Those who have clean hands and a pure heart,*
   who have not pledged themselves to falsehood,
   nor sworn by what is a fraud.
They shall receive a blessing from the LORD*
   and a just reward from the God of their salvation."
Such is the generation of those who seek him,*
   of those who seek your face, O God of Jacob.

Lift up your heads, O gates;
lift them high, O everlasting doors;*
   and the King of glory shall come in.
"Who is this King of glory?"*
   "The LORD, strong and mighty,
   the LORD, mighty in battle."
Lift up your heads, O gates;
lift them high, O everlasting doors;*
   and the King of glory shall come in.
"Who is he, this King of glory?"*
   "The LORD of hosts,
   he is the King of glory."

Psalm 46.   God, the source of peace

God is our refuge and strength,*
   a very present help in trouble.
Therefore we will not fear, though the earth be moved,*
   and though the mountains be toppled into the
                              depths of the sea;
Though its waters rage and foam,*
   and though the mountains tremble at its tumult.
The LORD of hosts is with us;*
   the God of Jacob is our stronghold.

There is a river whose streams make glad the city of God,*
   the holy habitation of the Most High.
God is in the midst of her;
she shall not be overthrown;*
   God shall help her at the break of day.
The nations make much ado, and the kingdoms are shaken;*
   God has spoken, and the earth shall melt away.
The LORD of hosts is with us;*
   the God of Jacob is our stronghold.

Come now and look upon the works of the LORD,*
   what awesome things he has done on earth.
It is he who makes war to cease in all the world;*
   he breaks the bow, and shatters the spear,
   and burns the shields with fire.

"Be still, then, and know that I am God;*
  I will be exalted among the nations;
  I will be exalted in the earth."
The Lord of hosts is with us;*
  the God of Jacob is our stronghold.

Psalm 51:1-18.   Prayer for mercy and for God's Spirit

Have mercy on me, O God, according to your
                            loving-kindness;*
  in your great compassion blot out my offenses.
Wash me through and through from my wickedness*
  and cleanse me from my sin.
For I know my transgressions,*
  and my sin is ever before me.
Against you only have I sinned*
  and done what is evil in your sight.
And so you are justified when you speak*
  and upright in your judgment.
Indeed, I have been wicked from my birth,*
  a sinner from my mother's womb.
For behold, you look for truth deep within me,*
  and will make me understand wisdom secretly.
Purge me from my sin, and I shall be pure;*
  wash me, and I shall be clean indeed.
Make me hear of joy and gladness,*
  that the body you have broken may rejoice.
Hide your face from my sins*
  and blot out all my iniquities.
Create in me a clean heart, O God,*
  and renew a right spirit within me.
Cast me not away from your presence*
  and take not your holy Spirit from me.
Give me the joy of your saving help again*
  and sustain me with your bountiful Spirit.
I shall teach your ways to the wicked,*
  and sinners shall return to you.

Deliver me from death, O God,*
 and my tongue shall sing of your righteousness,
 O God of my salvation.
Open my lips, O LORD,*
 and my mouth shall proclaim your praise.
Had you desired it, I would have offered sacrifice,*
 but you take no delight in burnt-offerings.
The sacrifice of God is a troubled spirit,*
 a broken and contrite heart, O God, you will not despise.

Psalm 63:1-8. Hunger and thirst for God

O God, you are my God; eagerly I seek you;*
 my soul thirsts for you, my flesh faints for you,
 as in a barren and dry land where there is no water.
Therefore I have gazed upon you in your holy place,*
 that I might behold your power and your glory.
For your loving-kindness is better than life itself;*
 my lips shall give you praise.
So will I bless you as long as I live*
 and lift up my hands in your Name.
My soul is content, as with marrow and fatness,*
 and my mouth praises you with joyful lips,
When I remember you upon my bed,*
 and meditate on you in the night watches.
For you have been my helper,*
 and under the shadow of your wings I will rejoice.
My soul clings to you;*
 your right hand holds me fast.

Psalm 65. Thanksgiving for God's blessings

You are to be praised, O God, in Zion;*
 to you shall vows be performed in Jerusalem.
To you that hear prayer shall all flesh come,*
 because of their transgressions.
Our sins are stronger than we are,*
 but you will blot them out.

Happy are they whom you choose
and draw to your courts to dwell there!*
    they will be satisfied by the beauty of your house,
    by the holiness of your temple.
Awesome things will you show us in your righteousness,
O God of our salvation,*
    O Hope of all the ends of the earth
    and of the seas that are far away.
You make fast the mountains by your power;*
    they are girded about with might.
You still the roaring of the seas,*
    the roaring of their waves,
    and the clamor of the peoples.
Those who dwell at the ends of the earth will tremble at your
                                    marvelous signs;*
    you make the dawn and the dusk to sing for joy.
You visit the earth and water it abundantly;
you make it very plenteous;*
    the river of God is full of water.
You prepare the grain,*
    for so you provide for the earth.
You drench the furrows and smooth out the ridges;*
    with heavy rain you soften the ground and bless its increase.
You crown the year with your goodness,*
    and your paths overflow with plenty.
May the fields of the wilderness be rich for grazing,*
    and the hills be clothed with joy.
May the meadows cover themselves with flocks,
and the valleys cloak themselves with grain;*
    let them shout for joy and sing.

Psalm 67. Song of blessing

May God be merciful to us and bless us,*
    show us the light of his countenance and come to us.
Let your ways be known upon earth,*
    your saving health among all nations.
Let the peoples praise you, O God;*
    let all the peoples praise you.

Let the nations be glad and sing for joy,*
  for you judge the peoples with equity
  and guide all the nations upon earth.
Let the peoples praise you, O God;*
  let all the peoples praise you.
The earth has brought forth her increase;*
  may God, our own God, give us his blessing.
May God give us his blessing,*
  and may all the ends of the earth stand in awe of him.

Psalm 84. Longing for God's dwelling

How dear to me is your dwelling, O LORD of hosts!*
  My soul has a desire and longing for the courts of
                        the LORD;
  my heart and my flesh rejoice in the living God.
The sparrow has found her a house
and the swallow a nest where she may lay her young;*
  by the side of your altars, O LORD of hosts,
  my King and my God.
Happy are they who dwell in your house!*
  they will always be praising you.
Happy are the people whose strength is in you!*
  whose hearts are set on the pilgrims' way.
Those who go through the desolate valley will find
                        it a place of springs,*
  for the early rains have covered it with pools of water.
They will climb from height to height,*
  and the God of gods will reveal himself in Zion.
LORD God of hosts, hear my prayer,*
  hearken, O God of Jacob.
Behold our defender, O God;*
  and look upon the face of your Anointed.
For one day in your courts is better than
                        a thousand in my own room,*
  and to stand at the threshold of the house of my God
  than to dwell in the tents of the wicked.
For the LORD God is both sun and shield;*
  he will give grace and glory;

No good thing will the LORD withhold*
  from those who walk with integrity.
O LORD of hosts,*
  happy are they who put their trust in you!

Psalm 85:8-13.   God's word of peace

I will listen to what the LORD God is saying,*
  for he is speaking peace to his faithful people
  and to those who turn their hearts to him.
Truly, his salvation is very near to those who fear him,*
  that his glory may dwell in our land.
Mercy and truth have met together;*
  righteousness and peace have kissed each other.
Truth shall spring up from the earth,*
  and righteousness shall look down from heaven.
The LORD will indeed grant prosperity,*
  and our land will yield its increase.
Righteousness shall go before him,*
  and peace shall be a pathway for his feet.

Psalm 95:1-7.   A call to worship

Come, let us sing to the LORD;*
  let us shout for joy to the Rock of our salvation.
Let us come before his presence with thanksgiving*
  and raise a loud shout to him with psalms.
For the LORD is a great God,*
  and a great King above all gods.
In his hand are the caverns of the earth,*
  and the heights of the hills are his also.
The sea is his, for he made it,*
  and his hands have molded the dry land.
Come, let us bow down, and bend the knee,*
  and kneel before the LORD our Maker.
For he is our God,
and we are the people of his pasture and the sheep of his hand.*
  Oh, that today you would hearken to his voice!

Psalm 98.   God, victor and judge

Sing to the LORD a new song,*
  for he has done marvelous things.
With his right hand and his holy arm*
  has he won for himself the victory.
The LORD has made known his victory;*
  his righteousness has he openly shown in
                the sight of the nations.
He remembers his mercy and faithfulness to
                the house of Israel,*
  and all the ends of the earth have seen the
                victory of our God.
Shout with joy to the LORD, all you lands;*
  lift up your voice, rejoice, and sing.
Sing to the LORD with the harp,*
  with the harp and the voice of song.
With trumpets and the sound of the horn*
  shout with joy before the King, the LORD.
Let the sea make a noise and all that is in it,*
  the lands and those who dwell therein.
Let the rivers clap their hands,*
  and let the hills ring out with joy before the LORD,
  when he comes to judge the earth.
In righteousness shall he judge the world*
  and the peoples with equity.

Psalm 100.   God, creator and shepherd

Be joyful in the LORD, all you lands;*
  serve the LORD with gladness
  and come before his presence with a song.
Know this: The LORD himself is God;*
  he himself has made us, and we are his;
  we are his people and the sheep of his pasture.
Enter his gates with thanksgiving;
go into his courts with praise;*
  give thanks to him and call upon his Name.

For the LORD is good;
his mercy is everlasting;*
   and his faithfulness endures from age to age.

Psalm 103. Praise for God's mercy

Bless the LORD, O my soul,*
   and all that is within me, bless his holy Name.
Bless the LORD, O my soul,*
   and forget not all his benefits.
He forgives all your sins*
   and heals all your infirmities;
He redeems your life from the grave*
   and crowns you with mercy and loving-kindness;
He satisfies you with good things,*
   and your youth is renewed like an eagle's.
The LORD executes righteousness*
   and judgment for all who are oppressed.
He made his ways known to Moses*
   and his works to the children of Israel.
The LORD is full of compassion and mercy,*
   slow to anger and of great kindness.
He will not always accuse us,*
   nor will he keep his anger for ever.
He has not dealt with us according to our sins,*
   nor rewarded us according to our wickedness.
For as the heavens are high above the earth,*
   so is his mercy great upon those who fear him.
As far as the east is from the west,*
   so far has he removed our sins from us.
As a father cares for his children,*
   so does the LORD care for those who fear him.
For he himself knows whereof we are made;*
   he remembers that we are but dust.
Our days are like the grass;*
   we flourish like a flower of the field;
When the wind goes over it, it is gone,*
   and its place shall know it no more.

But the merciful goodness of the LORD endures for ever
on those who fear him,*
  and his righteousness on children's children;
On those who keep his covenant*
  and remember his commandments and do them.
The LORD has set his throne in heaven,*
  and his kingship has dominion over all.
Bless the LORD, you angels of his,
you mighty ones who do his bidding,*
  and hearken to the voice of his word.
Bless the LORD, all you his hosts,*
  you ministers of his who do his will.
Bless the LORD, all you works of his,
in all places of his dominion;*
  bless the LORD, O my soul.

Psalm 114. The wonders of the Exodus

Hallelujah!
When Israel came out of Egypt,*
  the house of Jacob from a people of strange speech,
Judah became God's sanctuary*
  and Israel his dominion.
The sea beheld it and fled;*
  Jordan turned and went back.
The mountains skipped like rams,*
  and the little hills like young sheep.
What ailed you, O sea, that you fled?*
  O Jordan, that you turned back?
You mountains, that you skipped like rams?*
  you little hills like young sheep?
Tremble, O earth, at the presence of the Lord,*
  at the presence of the God of Jacob,
Who turned the hard rock into a pool of water*
  and flint-stone into a flowing spring.

Psalm 118:1-6, 19-24. Thanksgiving for salvation

Give thanks to the LORD for he is good;*
  his mercy endures for ever.
Let Israel now proclaim,*
  "His mercy endures for ever."
Let the house of Aaron now proclaim,*
  "His mercy endures for ever."
Let those who fear the LORD now proclaim,*
  "His mercy endures for ever."
I called to the LORD in my distress;*
  the LORD answered by setting me free.
The LORD is at my side, therefore I will not fear;*
  what can anyone do to me?
Open for me the gates of righteousness;*
  I will enter them;
  I will offer thanks to the LORD.
"This is the gate of the LORD;*
  he who is righteous may enter."
I will give thanks to you, for you answered me*
  and have become my salvation.
The same stone which the builders rejected*
  has become the chief cornerstone.
This is the LORD's doing,*
  and it is marvelous in our eyes.
On this day the LORD has acted;*
  we will rejoice and be glad in it.

Psalm 121. God our guardian

I lift up my eyes to the hills;*
  from where is my help to come?
My help comes from the LORD,*
  the maker of heaven and earth.
He will not let your foot be moved*
  and he who watches over you will not fall asleep.

Behold, he who keeps watch over Israel*
  shall neither slumber nor sleep;
The LORD himself watches over you;*
  the LORD is your shade at your right hand,
So that the sun shall not strike you by day,*
  nor the moon by night.
The LORD shall preserve you from all evil;*
  it is he who shall keep you safe.
The LORD shall watch over your going out and
                      your coming in,*
  from this time forth for evermore.

Psalm 122.   Jerusalem, a symbol of the Church

I was glad when they said to me,*
  "Let us go to the house of the LORD."
Now our feet are standing*
  within your gates, O Jerusalem.
Jerusalem is built as a city*
  that is at unity with itself;
To which the tribes go up,
the tribes of the LORD,*
  the assembly of Israel,
    to praise the Name of the LORD.
For there are the thrones of judgment,*
  the thrones of the house of David.
Pray for the peace of Jerusalem:*
  "May they prosper who love you.
Peace be within your walls*
  and quietness within your towers.
For my brethren and companions' sake,*
  I pray for your prosperity.
Because of the house of the LORD our God,*
  I will seek to do you good."

Psalm 130.   A cry from the depths

Out of the depths have I called to you, O LORD;
LORD, hear my voice;*
   let your ears consider well the voice of my supplication.
If you, LORD, were to note what is done amiss,*
   O LORD, who could stand?
For there is forgiveness with you;*
   therefore you shall be feared.
I wait for the LORD; my soul waits for him;*
   in his word is my hope.
My soul waits for the LORD,
more than watchmen for the morning,*
   more than watchmen for the morning.
O Israel, wait for the LORD,*
   for with the LORD there is mercy;
With him there is plenteous redemption,*
   and he shall redeem Israel from all their sins.

Psalm 139:1-11, 22-23.   The all-knowing and ever-present God

LORD, you have searched me out and known me;*
   you know my sitting down and my rising up;
   you discern my thoughts from afar.
You trace my journeys and my resting-places*
   and are acquainted with all my ways.
Indeed, there is not a word on my lips,*
   but you, O LORD, know it altogether.
You press upon me behind and before*
   and lay your hand upon me.
Such knowledge is too wonderful for me;*
   it is so high that I cannot attain to it.
Where can I go then from your Spirit?*
   where can I flee from your presence?
If I climb up to heaven, you are there;*
   if I make the grave my bed, you are there also.
If I take the wings of the morning*
   and dwell in the uttermost parts of the sea,

Even there your hand will lead me*
    and your right hand hold me fast.
If I say, "Surely the darkness will cover me,*
    and the light around me turn to night,"
Darkness is not dark to you;
the night is as bright as the day;*
    darkness and light to you are both alike.
Search me out, O God, and know my heart;*
    try me and know my restless thoughts.
Look well whether there be any wickedness in me*
    and lead me in the way that is everlasting.

Psalm 146. Hymn to God our helper

Hallelujah!
Praise the LORD, O my soul!*
    I will praise the LORD as long as I live;
    I will sing praises to my God while I have my being.
Put not your trust in rulers, nor in any child of earth,*
    for there is no help in them.
When they breathe their last, they return to earth,*
    and in that day their thoughts perish.
Happy are they who have the God of Jacob for their help!*
    whose hope is in the LORD their God;
Who made heaven and earth, the seas, and all that is in them;*
    who keeps his promise for ever;
Who gives justice to those who are oppressed,*
    and food to those who hunger.
The LORD sets the prisoners free;
the LORD opens the eyes of the blind;*
    the LORD lifts up those who are bowed down;
The LORD loves the righteous;
the LORD cares for the stranger,*
    he sustains the orphan and widow,
    but frustrates the way of the wicked.
The LORD shall reign for ever,*
    your God, O Zion, throughout all generations.
    Hallelujah!

Psalm 150. Praise from all creatures

Hallelujah!
Praise God in his holy temple;*
  praise him in the firmament of his power.
Praise him for his mighty acts;*
  praise him for his excellent greatness.
Praise him with the blast of the ram's-horn;*
  praise him with lyre and harp.
Praise him with timbrel and dance;*
  praise him with strings and pipe.
Praise him with resounding cymbals;*
  praise him with loud-clanging cymbals.
Let everything that has breath*
  praise the Lord.
  Hallelujah!

Canticles

1. You are God (*Te Deum laudamus*)

Commonly used in the morning, especially on Sundays and Feast Days.
It is also used as a hymn of thanksgiving on special occasions.

You are God: we praise you;
You are the Lord: we acclaim you;
You are the eternal Father:
All creation worships you.
To you all angels, all the powers of heaven,
Cherubim and Seraphim, sing in endless praise:
  Holy, holy, holy Lord, God of power and might,
  heaven and earth are full of your glory.
The glorious company of apostles praise you.
The noble fellowship of prophets praise you.
The white-robed army of martyrs praise you.
Throughout the world the holy Church acclaims you;
  Father, of majesty unbounded,
  your true and only Son, worthy of all worship,
  and the Holy Spirit, advocate and guide.

You, Christ, are the king of glory,
the eternal Son of the Father.
When you became man to set us free
you did not shun the Virgin's womb.
You overcame the sting of death
and opened the kingdom of heaven to all believers.
You are seated at God's right hand in glory.
We believe that you will come and be our judge.
    Come then, Lord, and help your people,
    bought with the price of your own blood,
    and bring us with your saints
    to glory everlasting.

2. A Song to the Lamb (*Dignus es*)
Revelation 4:11; 5:9-10, 13

Commonly used in the morning, especially on weekdays.

Splendor and honor and kingly power*
    are yours by right, O Lord our God,
For you created everything that is,
    and by your will they were created and have their being;

And yours by right, O Lamb that was slain,*
    for with your blood you have redeemed for God,
From every family, language, people, and nation,*
    a kingdom of priests to serve our God.

And so, to him who sits upon the throne,*
    and to Christ the Lamb,
Be worship and praise, dominion and splendor,*
    for ever and for evermore.

3. Glory to God (*Gloria in excelsis*)

Commonly used in the morning and at the Eucharist, but not in Advent and Lent.

See page 37.

4. O Gracious Light (*Phos hilaron*)

Used at the beginning of evening services.

See page 5.

5. The Song of Mary (*Magnificat*)
Luke 1:46-55

Commonly used in the evening.

My soul proclaims the greatness of the Lord,
my spirit rejoices in God my Savior,*
   for he has looked with favor on his lowly servant.
From this day all generations will call me blessed:*
   the Almighty has done great things for me,
   and holy is his Name.
He has mercy on those who fear him*
   in every generation.
He has shown the strength of his arm,*
   he has scattered the proud in their conceit.
He has cast down the mighty from their thrones,*
   and has lifted up the lowly.
He has filled the hungry with good things,*
   and the rich he has sent away empty.
He has come to the help of his servant Israel,*
   for he has remembered his promise of mercy,
The promise he made to our fathers,*
   to Abraham and his children for ever.

Glory to the Father, and to the Son, and to the Holy Spirit:*
   as it was in the beginning, is now, and will be for ever. Amen.

6. The Song of Simeon (*Nunc dimittis*)
Luke 2:29-32

Commonly used in the evening, or after Holy Communion.

See page 6.

Salmos

Salmo 23. El buen pastor

El Señor es mi pastor;*
   nada me faltará.
En verdes pastos me hace yacer;*
   me conduce hacia aguas tranquilas.
Aviva mi alma*
   y me guía por sendas seguras por amor de su Nombre.
Aunque ande en valle de sombra de muerte,
no temeré mal alguno;*
   porque tú estás conmigo;
   tu vara y tu cayado me infunden aliento.
Aderezarás mesa delante de mí
en presencia de mis angustiadores;*
   unges mi cabeza con óleo;
   mi copa está rebosando.
Ciertamente el bien y la misericordia me seguirán
todos los días de mi vida,*
   y en la casa del Señor moraré por largos días.

Salmo 98. Dios, victorioso y juez

Canten al Señor cántico nuevo,*
   porque ha hecho maravillas.
Con su diestra, y con su santo brazo,*
   ha alcanzado la victoria.
El Señor ha dado a conocer su victoria;*
   a la vista de las naciones ha descubierto su justicia.
Se acuerda de su misericordia y su fidelidad
para con la casa de Israel;*
   los confines de la tierra
                  han visto la victoria de nuestro Dios.
Aclamen con júbilo al Señor, pueblos todos;*
   levanten la voz, gócense y canten.
Canten al Señor con el arpa,*
   con el arpa y la voz de cántico.
Con trompetas y al son de clarines,*
   aclamen con júbilo ante el Rey, el Señor.

Ruja el mar y cuanto contiene,*
  el mundo y los que en él habitan.
Den palmadas los ríos, aclamen los montes al Señor,*
  cuando llegue para juzgar la tierra.
Juzgará al mundo con justicia,*
  y a los pueblos con equidad.

Salmo 118:1-6, 19-24. Acción de gracias por la salvación

Den gracias al Señor, porque él es bueno;*
  para siempre es su misericordia.
Diga ahora Israel:*
  "Para siempre es su misericordia".
Diga ahora la casa de Aarón:*
  "Para siempre es su misericordia".
Digan ahora los que veneran al Señor:*
  "Para siempre es su misericordia".
En mi angustia invoqué al Señor;*
  me respondió el Señor, poniéndome a salvo.
El Señor está a mi lado; por tanto, no temeré;*
  ¿quién podrá dañarme?
Abranme las puertas de justicia;*
  entraré por ellas, y daré gracias al Señor.
"Esta es la puerta del Señor;*
  por ella entrarán los justos".
Daré gracias porque me respondiste,*
  y me has sido de salvación.
La misma piedra que desecharon los edificadores,*
  ha venido a ser la cabeza del ángulo.
Esto es lo que ha hecho el Señor,*
  y es maravilloso a nuestro ojos.
Estes ës el día en que actuó el Señor;*
  regocijémonos y alegrémonos en él.

Salmo 130. Un clamor de lo profundo

De lo profundo, oh Señor, a ti clamo;
Señor, escucha mi voz;*
    estén atentos tus oídos a la voz de mi súplica.
Si tú, oh Señor, notares los delitos,*
    ¿quién, oh Señor, podrá mantenerse?
Mas en ti hay perdón,*
    por tanto serás venerado.
Aguardo al Señor; le aguarda mi alma;*
    en su palabra está mi esperanza.
Mi alma aguarda al Señor
más que los centinelas a la aurora,*
    más que los centinelas a la aurora.
Oh Israel, aguarda al Señor,*
    porque en el Señor hay misericordia;
Con él hay abundante redención,*
    y él redimirá a Israel de todos sus pecados.

Salmo 139: 1-11, 22-23 El Dios sapiente y omnipresente

Oh Señor, tú me has probado y conocido;*
    conoces mi sentarme y mi levantarme;
    percibes de lejos mis pensamientos.
Observas mis viajes y mis lugares de reposo,*
    y todos mis caminos te son conocidos.
Aún no está la palabra en mis labios,*
    y he aquí, oh Señor, tú la conoces.
Me rodeas delante y detrás,*
    y sobre mí pones tu mano.
Tal conocimiento es demasiado maravilloso para mí;*
    sublime es, y no lo puedo alcanzar.
¿A dónde huiré de tu Espíritu?*
    ¿A dónde huiré de tu presencia?
Si subiere a los cielos, allí estás tú
    si en el abismo hiciere mi lecho, allí estás también.
Si tomare las alas del alba,*
    y habitare en el extremo del mar,
Aun allí me guiará tu mano,*
    y me asirá tu diestra.

Si dijere: "Ciertamente las tinieblas me encubrirán,*
   y aun la luz se hará noche alrededor de mí",
Las tinieblas no son oscuras para ti;
la noche resplandece como el día;*
   lo mismo te son las tinieblas que la luz.
Escudríñame, oh Dios, y conoce mi corazón;*
   pruébame, y conoce mis inquietudes.
Ve si hay en mí camino de perversidad,*
   y guíame en el camino eterno.

Salmo 146. Himno a Dios nuestra ayuda

¡Aleluya!
Alaba, alma mía, al Señor;*
   alabaré al Señor mientras viva;
   cantaré alabanzas a mi Dios mientras exista.
No confíes en los príncipes, ni en ningún hijo de Adán,*
   porque no hay en ellos seguridad.
Al exhalar el espíritu, vuelven al polvo,*
   y en ese día perecen todos sus planes.
¡Dichosos aquéllos cuya ayuda es el Dios de Jacob,*
   cuya esperanza está en el Señor su Dios!
El cual hizo los cielos y la tierra,
el mar, y cuanto en ellos hay,*
   que guarda su promesa para siempre;
Que hace justicia a los oprimidos,*
   y da pan a los hambrientos.
El Señor liberta a los cautivos;
el Señor abre los ojos a los ciegos;*
   el Señor levanta a los caídos;
El Señor ama a los justos;
el Señor protege a los forasteros;*
   sostiene al huérfano y a la viuda,
   pero trastorna el camino de los malvados.
Reinará el Señor para siempre,*
   tu Dios, oh Sión, de generación en generación.
   ¡Aleluya!

Bible Readings

BIBLE READINGS

The readings given here are intended primarily for private devotion. They have been selected to help you understand more fully the wonderful things that God has done for us and for our salvation.

When meditating on Scripture, it is helpful to (1) ask God to open your heart to hear his word, (2) read the passage slowly, stopping whenever you want to think about what is being said, (3) resolve to practice in your life what you have learned from the reading, and (4) thank God for what he has taught you and pray for help to live by that teaching.

Because of the size of this book, only a few readings from the Old Testament could be included. As background to these stories, you may want to read the following passages from a Bible: Genesis, chapters 1, 6, 7, 8, 15; Exodus, chapters 2, 3, 12, 14, 19, 20; 1 Kings 8; 2 Kings 17; 2 Chronicles 36; Ezra 3; Isaiah 55.

A PRAYER FOR UNDERSTANDING HOLY SCRIPTURE

Blessed Lord, who caused all holy Scriptures to be written for our learning: Grant us so to hear them, read, mark, learn, and inwardly digest them, that we may embrace and ever hold fast the blessed hope of everlasting life, which you have given us in our Savior Jesus Christ; who lives and reigns with you and the Holy Spirit, one God, for ever and ever. *Amen.*

A GUIDE TO THE BIBLE READINGS

FOR THE CHURCH YEAR

Advent 9, 13, 23, 40

Christmas 10, 11

Epiphany 10, 12

Sundays after Epiphany 1, 12, 13, 14, 17, 19, 33, 34, 37

Lent 2, 3, 4, 5, 7, 8, 15, 16, 20, 25, 26, 35

Good Friday 26

Easter Season 27, 28, 21, 24, 38, 39, 40

Ascension Day 29, 30

The Day of Pentecost 5, 31

Trinity Sunday 1, 29

Other Sundays after Pentecost *Any reading may be chosen*

Saint's Days and Other Feasts 14, 23, 29, 38, 39, 41

National Days 3, 14, 22

FOR PARTICULAR NEEDS

Baptism and Confirmation 4, 5, 8, 12, 13, 14, 19, 29

Burial and Memorial Services 20, 21, 24, 38, 39, 41

The Christian Hope 20, 24, 38, 39

In Emergencies – see pages 34, 70

Holy Communion, Preparation for 6, 14, 20, 22, 25, 32, 35

Marriage 1, 14, 18, 19, 34, 35

Repentance and Forgiveness 8, 15, 28, 35, 36, 37

Sickness 16, 37, 38

1. God creates the universe and the human race

In the beginning God created the heavens and the earth. The earth was without form and void, and darkness was upon the face of the deep; and the Spirit of God was moving over the face of the waters.

And God said, "Let there be light"; and there was light. And God saw that the light was good; and God separated the light from the darkness. God called the light Day, and the darkness he called Night. And there was evening and there was morning, one day. . . .

[And on the sixth day] God said, "Let us make man in our image, after our likeness; and let them have dominion over the fish of the sea, and over the birds of the air, and over the cattle, and over all the earth, and over every creeping thing that creeps upon the earth." So God created man in his own image, in the image of God he created him; male and female he created them. And God blessed them, and God said to them, "Be fruitful and multiply, and fill the earth and subdue it." And it was so. And God saw everything that he had made, and behold, it was very good. *Genesis 1:1-5, 26-28a, 30b-31a.*

2. The human race becomes corrupt

The Lord saw that the wickedness of man was great in the earth, and that every imagination of the thoughts of his heart was only evil continually. And the Lord was sorry that he had made man on the earth, and it grieved him to his heart. So the Lord said, "I will blot out man whom I have created from the face of the ground, man and beast and creeping things and birds of the air, for I am sorry that I ever made them." But Noah found favor in the eyes of the Lord. And God said to Noah, "I have determined to make an end of all flesh; for the earth is filled with violence through them; behold, I will destroy them with the earth. Make yourself an ark of gopher wood; make rooms in the ark, and cover it inside and out with pitch. For behold, I will bring a flood of waters upon the earth, to destroy all flesh in which is the breath of life from under heaven; everything that is on the earth shall die. But I will establish my covenant with you; and you shall come into the ark, you, your sons, your wife, and your sons' wives with you." *Genesis 6:5-8, 13-14, 17-18.*

3. God makes a promise to Abraham

The Lord appeared to Abram, and said to him, "I am God Almighty; walk before me, and be blameless. And I will make my covenant between me and you, and will multiply you exceedingly." Then Abram fell on his face; and God said to him, "Behold, my covenant is with you, and you shall be the father of a multitude of nations. No longer shall your name be Abram, but your name shall be Abraham; for I have made you exceedingly fruitful; and I will make nations of you, and kings shall come forth from you. And I will establish my covenant between me and you and your descendants after you throughout their generations for an everlasting covenant, to be God to you and to your descendants after you. And I will give to you, and to your descendants after you, the land of your sojournings, all the land of Canaan, for an everlasting possession; and I will be their God." *Genesis 17:1-8.*

4. God rescues the Children of Israel

In the morning watch the Lord in the pillar of fire and of cloud looked down upon the host of the Egyptians, and discomfited the host of the Egyptians, clogging their chariot wheels so that they drove heavily; and the Egyptians said, "Let us flee from before Israel; for the Lord fights for them against the Egyptians."

Then the Lord said to Moses, "Stretch out your hand over the sea, that the water may come back upon the Egyptians, upon their chariots, and upon their horsemen." So Moses stretched forth his hand over the sea, and the sea returned to its wonted flow when the morning appeared; and the Egyptians fled into it, and the Lord routed the Egyptians in the midst of the sea. The waters returned and covered the chariots and the horsemen and all the host of Pharaoh that had followed them into the sea; not so much as one of them remained. But the people of Israel walked on dry ground through the sea, the waters being a wall to them on their right hand and on their left.

Thus the Lord saved Israel that day from the hand of the Egyptians; and Israel saw the Egyptians dead upon the seashore. And Israel saw the great work which the Lord did against the Egyptians, and the people feared the Lord; and they believed in the Lord and in his servant Moses. *Exodus 14:24-31.*

5. God makes a covenant with Israel

After the people of Israel had gone forth out of the land of Egypt, on the third new moon they came into the wilderness of Sinai. And Moses went up to God, and the Lord called to him out of the mountain, saying, "Thus you shall say to the house of Jacob, and tell the people of Israel: You have seen what I did to the Egyptians, and how I bore you on eagles' wings and brought you to myself. Now therefore, if you will obey my voice and keep my covenant, you shall be my own possession among all peoples; for all the earth is mine, and you shall be to me a kingdom of priests and a holy nation. These are the words which you shall speak to the children of Israel."

So Moses came and called the elders of the people, and set before them all these words which the Lord had commanded him. And all the people answered together and said, "All that the Lord has spoken we will do."   *Exodus 19:1, 3-8a.*

6. God gives Israel the Ten Commandments

See pages 57-58.

7. Israel is taken into exile

All the leading priests and the people of Judah and Jerusalem were exceedingly unfaithful, following all the abominations of the nations; and they polluted the house of the Lord which he had hallowed in Jerusalem.

The Lord, the God of their fathers, sent persistently to them by his messengers, because he had compassion on his people and on his dwelling place; but they kept mocking the messengers of God, despising his words, and scoffing at his prophets, till the wrath of the Lord rose against his people, till there was no remedy.

Therefore he brought up against them the king of the Chaldeans, who slew their young men with the sword in the house of their sanctuary, and had no compassion on young man or virgin, old man or aged; he gave them all into his hand. And they burned the house of God, and broke down the wall of Jerusalem, and burned all its palaces with fire, and destroyed all its precious vessels. He took into exile in Babylon those who had escaped from the sword, and they became servants to him and to his sons until the establishment of the kingdom of Persia, to fulfill the word of the Lord by the mouth of Jeremiah, until the land had enjoyed its sabbaths. All the days that it lay desolate it kept sabbath, to fulfill seventy years. *2 Chronicles 36:14-17, 19-21.*

8. God promises a new covenant

Behold, the days are coming, says the Lord, when I will make a new covenant with the house of Israel and the house of Judah, not like the covenant which I made with their fathers when I took them by the hand to bring them out of the land of Egypt, my covenant which they broke, though I was their husband, says the Lord. But this is the covenant which I will make with the house of Israel after those days, says the Lord: I will put my law within them, and I will write it upon their hearts; and I will be their God, and they shall be my people. And no longer shall each man teach his neighbor and each his brothers, saying, "Know the Lord," for they shall all know me, from the least of them to the greatest, says the Lord; for I will forgive their iniquity, and I will remember their sin no more. *Jeremiah 31:31-34.*

9. "Prepare the way of the Lord"

Comfort, comfort my people, says your God. Speak tenderly to Jerusalem, and cry to her that her warfare is ended, that her iniquity is pardoned, that she has received from the Lord's hand double for all her sins.

A voice cries, "In the wilderness prepare the way of the Lord, make straight in the desert a highway for our God. Every valley shall be lifted up, and every mountain and hill be made low; the uneven ground shall become level, and the rough places a plain. And the glory of the Lord shall be revealed, and all flesh shall see it together, for the mouth of the Lord has spoken.

Get you up to a high mountain, O Zion, herald of good tidings; lift up your voice with strength, O Jerusalem, herald of good tidings, lift it up, fear not; say to the cities of Judah, "Behold your God!" Behold, the Lord God comes with might, and his arm rules for him; behold, his reward is with him, and his recompense before him. He will feed his flock like a shepherd, he will gather the lambs in his arms, he will carry them in his bosom, and gently lead those that are with young. *Isaiah 40:1-5, 9-11.*

10. Prophecy of the Messianic King

The people who walked in darkness have seen a great light; those who dwelt in a land of deep darkness, on them has light shined. For to us a child is born, to us a son is given; and the government will be upon his shoulder, and his name will be called "Wonderful Counselor, Mighty God, Everlasting Father, Prince of Peace." Of the increase of his government and of peace there will be no end, upon the throne of David, and over his kingdom, to establish it, and to uphold it with justice and with righteousness from this time forth and for evermore. The zeal of the Lord of hosts will do this. *Isaiah 9:2, 6-7.*

11. Jesus Christ is born

In those days a decree went out from Caesar Augustus that all the world should be enrolled. This was the first enrollment, when Quirinius was governor of Syria. And all went to be enrolled, each to his own city. And Joseph also went up from Galilee, from the city of Nazareth, to Judea, to the city of David, which is called Bethlehem, because he was of the house and lineage of David, to be enrolled with Mary his betrothed, who was with child. And while they were there, the time came for her to be delivered. And she gave birth to her first-born son and wrapped him in swaddling cloths, and laid him in a manger, because there was no place for them in the inn.

And in that region there were shepherds out in the field, keeping watch over their flock by night. And an angel of the Lord appeared to them, and the glory of the Lord shone around them, and they were filled with fear. And the angel said to them, "Be not afraid; for behold, I bring you good news of a great joy which will come to all the people; for to you is born this day in the city of David a Savior, who is Christ the Lord. And this will be a sign for you: you will find a babe wrapped in swaddling cloths and lying in a manger. And suddenly there was with the angel a multitude of the heavenly host praising God and saying, "Glory to God in the highest, and on earth peace among men with whom he is pleased!" *Luke 2:1-14.*

12. Jesus is baptized

John the baptizer was preaching in the wilderness; and in those days Jesus came from Nazareth of Galilee and was baptized by John in the

Jordan. And when he came up out of the water, immediately he saw the heavens opened and the Spirit descending upon him like a dove; and a voice came from heaven, "Thou art my beloved Son; with thee I am well pleased." *Mark 1:9-11.*

Jesus preaches in the synagogue

Jesus came to Nazareth, where he had been brought up; and he went to the synagogue, as his custom was, on the sabbath day. And he stood up to read; and there was given to him the book of the prophet Isaiah. He opened the book and found the place where it was written, "The Spirit of the Lord is upon me, because he has anointed me to preach good news to the poor. He has sent me to proclaim release to the captives and recovering of sight to the blind, to set at liberty those who are oppressed, to proclaim the acceptable year of the Lord." And he closed the book, and gave it back to the attendant, and sat down; and the eyes of all in the synagogue were fixed on him. And he began to say to them, "Today this scripture has been fulfilled in your hearing." *Luke 4:16-21.*

14. Christ teaches the Beatitudes

Jesus went up on the mountain, and when he sat down his disciples came to him. And he opened his mouth and taught them, saying:

"Blessed are the poor in spirit, for theirs is the kingdom of heaven.

"Blessed are those who mourn, for they shall be comforted.

"Blessed are the meek, for they shall inherit the earth.

"Blessed are those who hunger and thirst for righteousness, for they shall be satisfied.

"Blessed are the merciful, for they shall obtain mercy.

"Blessed are the pure in heart, for they shall see God.

"Blessed are the peacemakers, for they shall be called children of God.

"Blessed are those who are persecuted for righteousness' sake, for theirs is the kingdom of heaven.

"Blessed are you when men revile you and persecute you and utter all kinds of evil against you falsely on my account. Rejoice and be glad, for your reward is great in heaven, for so men persecuted the prophets who were before you." *Matthew 5:1-12.*

15. Christ calls sinners

Levi the tax collector made a great feast for Jesus in his house; and there was a large company of tax collectors and others sitting at table with them. And the Pharisees and their scribes murmured against his disciples, saying, "Why do you eat and drink with tax collectors and sinners?" And Jesus answered them, "Those who are well have no need of a physician, but those who are sick; I have not come to call the righteous, but sinners to repentance." *Luke 5:29-32.*

16. Christ heals the sick

A ruler knelt before Jesus, saying, "My daughter has just died; but come and lay your hand on her, and she will live." And Jesus rose and followed him, with his disciples. And behold, a woman who had suffered from a hemorrhage for twelve years came up behind him and touched the fringe of his garment; for she said to herself, "If I only touch his garment, I shall be made well." Jesus turned, and seeing her he said, "Take heart, daughter; your faith has made you well." And instantly the woman was made well. And when Jesus came to the ruler's house, and saw the flute players, and the crowd making a tumult, he said, "Depart; for the girl is not dead but sleeping." And they laughed at him. But when the crowd had been put outside, he went in and took her by the hand, and the girl arose. And the report of this went through all that district. *Matthew 9:18-26.*

17. Christ's true family

The mother and brothers of Jesus came to his home, and standing outside they sent to him and called him. And a crowd was sitting about Jesus; and they said to him, "Your mother and your brothers are outside, asking for you." And he replied, "Who are my mother and my brothers?" And looking around on those who sat about him, he said, "Here are my mother and my brothers! Whoever does the will of God is my brother, and sister, and mother." *Mark 3:31-35.*

18. Christ's teaching on marriage

Jesus said, "From the beginning of creation, 'God made them male and female.' 'For this reason a man shall leave his father and mother and be joined to his wife, and the two shall become one flesh.' So they are no longer two but one flesh. What therefore God has joined together, let not man put asunder." *Mark 10:6-9.*

19. Christ welcomes children

People were bringing children to Jesus, that he might touch them; and the disciples rebuked them. But when Jesus saw it he was indignant, and said to them, "Let the children come to me, do not hinder them; for to such belongs the kingdom of God. Truly, I say to you, whoever does not receive the kingdom of God like a child shall not enter it." And Jesus took the children in his arms and blessed them, laying his hands upon them. *Mark 10:13-16.*

20. Christ is our food

Jesus said, "I am the bread of life; he who comes to me shall not hunger, and he who believes in me shall never thirst. He who eats my flesh and drinks my blood has eternal life, and I will raise him up at the last day. For my flesh is food indeed, and my blood is drink indeed. He who eats my flesh and drinks my blood abides in me, and I in him. As the living Father sent me, and I live because of the Father, so he who eats me will live because of me. This is the bread which came down from heaven, not such as the fathers ate and died; he who eats this bread will live for ever." *John 6:35, 54-58.*

21. The good shepherd

Jesus said to the Pharisees, "I am the door; if any one enters by me, he will be saved, and will go in and out and find pasture. The thief comes only to steal and kill and destroy; I came that they may have life, and have it abundantly. I am the good shepherd. The good shepherd lays down his life for the sheep. He who is a hireling and not a shepherd, whose own the sheep are not, sees the wolf coming and leaves the sheep and flees; and the wolf snatches them and scatters them. He flees because he is a hireling and cares nothing for the sheep. I am the good shepherd; I know my own and my own know me, as the Father knows me and I know the Father; and I lay down my life for the sheep. And I have other sheep, that are not of this fold; I must bring them also, and they will heed my voice. So there shall be one flock, one shepherd." *John 10:9-16.*

22. Christ's summary of the Law

See pages 57 and 58.

23. Serving Christ in others

Jesus, sitting on the Mount of Olives, said to his disciples, "The King will say to those at his right hand, 'Come, O blessed of my Father, inherit the kingdom prepared for you from the foundation of the world; for I was hungry and you gave me food, I was thirsty and you gave me drink, I was a stranger and you welcomed me, I was naked and you clothed me, I was sick and you visited me, I was in prison and you came to me.' Then the righteous will answer him, 'Lord, when did we see thee hungry and feed thee, or thirsty and give thee drink? And when did we see thee a stranger and welcome thee, or naked and clothe thee? And when did we see thee sick or in prison and visit thee?' And the King will answer them, 'Truly, I say to you, as you did it to one of the least of these my brethren, you did it to me.' "
Matthew 25:34-40.

24. Christ's promise to us

Jesus said to the disciples, "Let not your hearts be troubled; believe in God, believe also in me. In my Father's house are many rooms; if it were not so, would I have told you that I go to prepare a place for you? And when I go and prepare a place for you, I will come again and will take you to myself, that where I am you may be also. And you know the way where I am going." Thomas said to him, "Lord, we do not know where you are going; how can we know the way?" Jesus said to him, "I am the way, and the truth, and the life; no one comes to the Father, but by me." *John 14:1-6.*

25. The last supper

When the hour for the passover came, Jesus sat at table, and the apostles with him. And he said to them, "I have earnestly desired to eat this passover with you before I suffer." And he took bread, and when he had given thanks he broke it and gave it to them, saying, "This is my body which is given for you. Do this in remembrance of me." And likewise the cup after supper, saying, "This cup which is poured out for you is the new covenant in my blood." *Luke 22:14-15, 19-20.*

26. Jesus dies on the cross

The soldiers brought Jesus to the place called Golgotha (which means the place of a skull). And they offered him wine mingled with myrrh; but he did not take it. And they crucified him, and divided his garments among them, casting lots for them, to decide what each should take. And it was the third hour, when they crucified him. And the inscription of the charge against him read, "The King of the Jews." And with him they crucified two robbers, one on his right and one on his left. And those who passed by derided him, wagging their heads, and saying, "Aha! You who would destroy the temple and build it in three days, save yourself, and come down from the cross!" So also the chief priests mocked him to one another with the scribes, saying, "He saved others; he cannot save himself. Let the Christ, the King of Israel, come down now from the cross, that we may see and believe." Those who were crucified with him also reviled him.

And when the sixth hour had come, there was darkness over the whole land until the ninth hour. And at the ninth hour Jesus cried with a loud voice, "Elo-i, Elo-i, lama sabachthani?" which means, "My God, my God, why hast thou forsaken me?" And some of the bystanders hearing it said, "Behold, he is calling Elijah." And one ran and, filling a sponge full of vinegar, put it on a reed and gave it to him to drink, saying, "Wait, let us see whether Elijah will come to take him down." And Jesus uttered a loud cry, and breathed his last. And the curtain of the temple was torn in two, from top to bottom. And when the centurion, who stood facing him, saw that he thus breathed his last, he said, "Truly this man was the Son of God!" *Mark 15:22-39.*

27. The empty tomb

When the sabbath was past, Mary Magdalene, and Mary the mother of James, and Salome, bought spices, so that they might go and anoint him. And very early on the first day of the week they went to the tomb when the sun had risen. And they were saying to one another, "Who will roll away the stone for us from the door of the tomb?" And looking up, they saw that the stone was rolled back—it was very large. And entering the tomb, they saw a young man sitting on the right side, dressed in a white robe; and they were amazed. And he said to them, "Do not be amazed; you seek Jesus of Nazareth, who was crucified. He has risen, he is not here; see the place where they laid him. But go, tell his disciples and Peter that he is going before you to Galilee; there you will see him, as he told you." And they went out and fled from the tomb; for trembling and astonishment had come upon them; and they said nothing to any one, for they were afraid. *Mark 16:1-8.*

28. The Risen Christ appears

On the evening of the first day of the week, the doors being shut where the disciples were, for fear of the Jews, Jesus came and stood among them and said to them, "Peace be with you." When he had said this, he showed them his hands and his side. Then the disciples were glad when they saw the Lord. Jesus said to them again, "Peace be with you. As the Father has sent me, even so I send you." And when he had said this, he breathed on them, and said to them, "Receive the Holy Spirit. If you forgive the sins of any, they are forgiven; if you retain the sins of any, they are retained." *John 20:19-23.*

29. The great commission

Jesus came to his disciples and said, "All authority in heaven and on earth has been given to me. Go therefore and make disciples of all nations, baptizing them in the name of the Father and of the Son and of the Holy Spirit, teaching them to observe all that I have commanded you; and lo, I am with you always, to the close of the age."
Matthew 28:18-20.

30. Jesus ascends into heaven

When the disciples had come together with Jesus, he said, "You shall receive power when the Holy Spirit has come upon you; and you shall be my witnesses in Jerusalem and in all Judea and Samaria and to the end of the earth." And when he had said this, as they were looking on, he was lifted up, and a cloud took him out of their sight. And while they were gazing into heaven as he went, behold, two men stood by them in white robes, and said, "Men of Galilee, why do you stand look-

ing into heaven? This Jesus, who was taken up from you into heaven, will come in the same way as you saw him go into heaven."
Acts 1:8-11.

31. The Holy Spirit comes to the Church

When the day of Pentecost had come, the disciples were all together in one place. And suddenly a sound came from heaven like the rush of a mighty wind, and it filled all the house where they were sitting. And there appeared to them tongues as of fire, distributed and resting on each one of them. And they were all filled with the Holy Spirit and began to speak in other tongues, as the Spirit gave them utterance.

Now there were dwelling in Jerusalem Jews, devout men from every nation under heaven. And at this sound the multitude came together, and they were bewildered, because each one heard them speaking in his own language.

But Peter, standing with the eleven, lifted up his voice and addressed them, "Men of Israel, hear these words: Jesus of Nazareth, a man attested to you by God with mighty works and wonders and signs which God did through him in your midst, as you yourselves know—this Jesus, delivered up according to the definite plan and foreknowledge of God, you crucified and killed by the hands of lawless men. But God raised him up, having loosed the pangs of death, because it was not possible for him to be held by it.

"Being therefore exalted at the right hand of God, and having received from the Father the promise of the Holy Spirit, he has poured out this which you see and hear."

Now when they heard this they were cut to the heart, and said to Peter and the rest of the apostles, "Brethren, what shall we do?" And Peter said to them, "Repent, and be baptized every one of you in the name of Jesus Christ for the forgiveness of your sins; and you shall receive the gift of the Holy Spirit. For the promise is to you and to your children and to all that are far off, every one whom the Lord our God calls to him." So those who received his word were baptized, and there were added that day about three thousand souls. And they devoted themselves to the apostles' teaching and fellowship, to the breaking of bread and the prayers. *Acts 2:1-6, 14a, 22-24, 33, 37-39, 41-42.*

32. Christians are members of Christ's body

The cup of blessing which we bless, is it not a participation in the blood of Christ? The bread which we break, is it not a participation in the body of Christ? Because there is one bread, we who are many are one body, for we all partake of the one bread. *1 Corinthians 10:16-17.*

33. Paul explains the gifts of the Spirit

There are varieties of gifts, but the same Spirit; and there are varieties of service, but the same Lord; and there are varieties of working, but it is the same God who inspires them all in every one. To each is given the manifestation of the Spirit for the common good. To one is given through the Spirit the utterance of wisdom, and to another the utterance of knowledge according to the same Spirit, to another faith by the same Spirit, to another gifts of healing by the one Spirit, to another the working of miracles, to another prophecy, to another the ability to distinguish between spirits, to another various kinds of tongues, to another the interpretation of tongues. All these are inspired by one and the same Spirit, who apportions to each one individually as he wills.

For just as the body is one and has many members, and all the members of the body, though many, are one body, so it is with Christ. For by one Spirit we were all baptized into one body — Jews and Greeks, slaves or free — and all were made to drink of one Spirit.
1 Corinthians 12:4-13.

34. Christian love

Love is patient and kind; love is not jealous or boastful; it is not arrogant or rude. Love does not insist on its own way; it is not irritable or resentful; it does not rejoice at wrong, but rejoices in the right. Love bears all things, believes all things, hopes all things, endures all things. Love never ends. *1 Corinthians 13:4-8a.*

35. Christian conduct

Put on, as God's chosen ones, holy and beloved, compassion, kindness, lowliness, meekness, and patience, forbearing one another and, if one has a complaint against another, forgiving each other; as the Lord has forgiven you, so you also must forgive. And above all these put on love, which binds everything together in perfect harmony. And let the peace of Christ rule in your hearts, to which indeed you were called in the one body. And be thankful. *Colossians 3:12-15.*

36. Our merciful High Priest

Since we have a great high priest who has passed through the heavens, Jesus, the Son of God, let us hold fast our confession. For we have not a high priest who is unable to sympathize with our weaknesses, but one who in every respect has been tempted as we are, yet without sin. Let us then with confidence draw near to the throne of grace, that we may receive mercy and find grace to help in time of need. *Hebrews 4:14-16.*

37. The Church's ministry to the sick

Is any one among you suffering? Let him pray. Is any cheerful? Let him sing praise. Is any among you sick? Let him call for the presbyters of the church, and let them pray over him, anointing him with oil in the name of the Lord; and the prayer of faith will save the sick, and the Lord will raise him up; and if he has committed sins, he will be forgiven. Therefore confess your sins to one another, and pray for one another, that you may be healed. *James 5:13-16a.*

38. "Who shall separate us?"

Who shall separate us from the love of Christ? Shall tribulation, or distress, or persecution, or famine, or nakedness, or peril, or sword? No, in all these things we are more than conquerors through him who loved us. For I am sure that neither death, nor life, nor angels, nor principalities, nor things present, nor things to come, nor powers, nor height, nor depth, nor anything else in all creation, will be able to separate us from the love of God in Christ Jesus our Lord. *Romans 8:35, 37-39.*

39. The resurrection of the dead

Lo! I tell you a mystery. We shall not all sleep, but we shall all be changed, in a moment, in the twinkling of an eye, at the last trumpet. For the trumpet will sound, and the dead will be raised imperishable, and we shall be changed. For this perishable nature must put on the imperishable, and this mortal nature must put on immortality. When the perishable puts on the imperishable, and the mortal puts on immortality, then shall come to pass the saying that is written:

"Death is swallowed up in victory."

"O death, where is thy victory?"

O death, where is thy sting?"

The sting of death is sin, and the power of sin is the law. But thanks be to God, who gives us the victory through our Lord Jesus Christ. *1 Corinthians 15:51-57.*

40. Christ will come again

John to the seven churches that are in Asia: Grace to you and peace from him who is and who was and who is to come, and from the seven spirits who are before his throne, and from Jesus Christ the faithful witness, the first-born of the dead, and the ruler of kings on earth.

To him who loves us and has freed us from our sins by his blood and made us a kingdom, priests to his God and Father, to him be glory and dominion for ever and ever. Amen. Behold, he is coming with the clouds, and every eye will see him, every one who pierced him; and all tribes of the earth will wail on account of him. Even so. Amen.

"I am the Alpha and the Omega," says the Lord God, who is and who was and who is to come, the Almighty. *Revelation 1:4-8.*

41. "Behold, I make all things new"

I saw a new heaven and a new earth; for the first heaven and the first earth had passed away, and the sea was no more. And I saw the holy city, new Jerusalem, coming down out of heaven from God, prepared as a bride adorned for her husband; and I heard a loud voice from the throne saying, "Behold, the dwelling of God is with men. He will dwell with them, and they shall be his people, and God himself will be with them; he will wipe away every tear from their eyes, and death shall be no more, neither shall there be mourning nor crying nor pain any more, for the former things have passed away."

And he who sat upon the throne said, "Behold, I make all things new." *Revelation 21:1-5a.*

Prayers

PRAYERS

Like most Christians, Episcopalians frequently pray in words written by other people. There are many reasons for this. One is that such prayers sometimes say what we want to say better than we can say it ourselves. Another is that they suggest topics for prayer we might not have thought of, but which we are glad to make our own. Some written prayers are very old, and have been hallowed by the lips of millions of Christians through the centuries. Others are new, and express the concerns of the world today.

It is also important that we pray in our own words. Our prayer may be very simple. It may be long or short. The important thing is that we pray in faith. Ordinarily, Christian prayer is addressed to God (the Father) through Jesus Christ, and in the power of the Holy Spirit. We may also address our prayers directly to Jesus or to the Holy Spirit.

Most of the prayers in this section follow a pattern known as the "collect" form. Many people use this same form when making up their own prayers (although this is not necessary).

Most collects have the following structure:

1. *The address to God.* This may be very short, such as "O God," or it may be longer, such as "Merciful and loving God." Sometimes a phrase or clause is added to the address, such as "creator of heaven and earth" or "you are more willing to listen than we are to pray."

2. *The petition.* Here God is asked to do something for the person or persons praying or for others. Sometimes a reason for the prayer is added, such as "that all people may live in peace and safety" or "that we may love you more and serve you better."

3. *The conclusion.* This may be short, such as "we ask this through Jesus our Savior," or it may be long, such as "through Jesus Christ our Lord, who lives and reigns with you and the Holy Spirit, one God, for ever and ever. *Amen.*"

A GUIDE TO THE PRAYERS

For particular prayers, see the index on pages 159-166.

Collects for the Church Year are on pages 10-17.

In the prayers that follow (and throughout this book) the letters *N.* and *NN.* indicate where the name or names of the persons being referred to are to be inserted. The words *"he," "him,"* and *"his"* (in italics) should be changed to "she," "her," "hers," "they," "them," or "theirs" as appropriate.

1. For Joy in God's Creation

O heavenly Father, you have filled the world with beauty: Open our eyes to behold your gracious hand in all your works; that, rejoicing in your whole creation, we may learn to serve you with gladness; for the sake of him through whom all things were made, your Son Jesus Christ our Lord. *Amen.*

2. For Peace

Eternal God, in whose perfect kingdom no sword is drawn but the sword of righteousness, no strength known but the strength of love: So mightily spread abroad your Spirit, that all peoples may be gathered under the banner of the Prince of Peace, as children of one Father; to whom be dominion and glory, now and for ever. *Amen.*

3. For Peace Among the Nations

Almighty God our heavenly Father, guide the nations of the world into the way of justice and truth, and establish among them that peace which is the fruit of righteousness, that they may become the kingdom of our Lord and Savior Jesus Christ. *Amen.*

4. For our Enemies

O God, the Father of all, whose Son commanded us to love our enemies: Lead them and us from prejudice to truth; deliver them and us from hatred, cruelty, and revenge; and in your good time enable us all to stand reconciled before you; through Jesus Christ our Lord. *Amen.*

5. For the Unity of the Church

Almighty Father, whose blessed Son before his passion prayed for his disciples that they might be one, as you and he are one: Grant that your Church, being bound together in love and obedience to you, may be united in one body by the one Spirit, that the world may believe in him whom you have sent, your Son Jesus Christ our Lord. *Amen.*

6. For the Mission of the Church

O God, you have made of one blood all the peoples of the earth, and sent your blessed Son to preach peace to those who are far off and to those who are near: Grant that people everywhere may seek after you and find you; bring the nations into your fold; pour out your Spirit upon all flesh; and hasten the coming of your kingdom; through Jesus Christ our Lord. *Amen.*

7. For Those to be Baptized or Confirmed

O God, you prepared your disciples for the coming of the Spirit through the teaching of your Son Jesus Christ: Make the hearts and minds of your servants ready to receive the blessing of the Holy Spirit, that they may be filled with the strength of his presence; through Jesus Christ our Lord. *Amen.*

8. For our Country

Lord God Almighty, you have made all the peoples of the earth for your glory, to serve you in freedom and in peace: Give to the people of our country a zeal for justice and the strength of forbearance, that we may use our liberty in accordance with your gracious will; through Jesus Christ our Lord. *Amen.*

9. For the President

O Lord our Governor, whose glory is in all the world: We commend this nation to your merciful care, that, being guided by your Providence, we may dwell secure in your peace. Grant to the President of the United States, and to all in authority, wisdom and strength to know and to do your will. Fill them with the love of truth and righteousness, and make them ever mindful of their calling to serve this people in your fear; through Jesus Christ our Lord. *Amen.*

10. For the Armed Forces

Lord God of grace and power, stretch forth your almighty arm to strengthen and protect all those in the armed forces of our country. Support them in the day of battle, and in times of peace keep them safe from evil. Endue them with courage and loyalty, and grant that they may serve without reproach; through Jesus Christ our Lord. *Amen.*

11. For Social Justice

Almighty God, who created us in your own image: Grant us grace fearlessly to contend against evil and to make no peace with oppression; and, that we may reverently use our freedom, help us to employ it in the maintenance of justice in our communities and among the nations, to the glory of your holy Name; through Jesus Christ our Lord. *Amen.*

12. For the Poor and the Neglected

Almighty and most merciful God, we remember before you all poor and neglected persons whom it would be easy for us to forget: the homeless and the destitute, the old and the sick, and all who have none to care for them. Help us to heal those who are broken in body and spirit, and to turn their sorrow into joy. Grant this, Father, for the love of your Son, who for our sake became poor, Jesus Christ our Lord. *Amen.*

13. For the Hungry

Eternal God, who fed your people with manna in the wilderness: Look with pity on all those who today are hungry. Open our hearts and hands to help them, and inspire the leaders of the world to work for the welfare of all the people; through Jesus Christ our Lord. *Amen.*

14. For Prisoners

We beseech you, O God, for all prisoners and captives, and for all who suffer from oppression. Show them your mercy and love, we pray, and make the hearts of human beings as merciful as your own; through Jesus Christ our Lord. *Amen.*

15. For the Right Use of God's Gifts

Almighty God, whose loving hand has given us all that we possess: Grant us grace that we may honor you with our substance, and, remembering the account which we must one day give, may be faithful stewards of your bounty, through Jesus Christ our Lord. *Amen.*

16. For Married Persons

O gracious and everliving God, you have created us male and female in your image: Look mercifully upon N. and N. (*or* all married persons), and assist them with your grace, that with true fidelity and steadfast love they may honor and keep the promises and vows they have made to each other; through Jesus Christ our Lord. *Amen.*

17. For the Care of Children

Almighty God, heavenly Father, you have blessed us with the joy and care of children: Give us calm strength and patient wisdom as we bring them up, that we may teach them to love whatever is just and true and good, following the example of our Savior Jesus Christ. *Amen.*

18. For Young Persons

God our Father, you see your children growing up in an unsteady and confusing world: Show them that your ways give more life than the ways of the world, and that following you is better than chasing after selfish goals. Help them to take failure, not as a measure of their worth, but as a chance for a new start. Give them strength to hold their faith in you, and to keep alive their joy in your creation; through Jesus Christ our Lord. *Amen.*

19. For a Birthday

O God, our times are in your hand: Look with favor, we pray, on your servant N. as *he* begins another year. Grant that *he* may grow in wisdom and grace, and strengthen *his* trust in your goodness all the days of *his* life; through Jesus Christ our Lord. *Amen.*

20. For the Absent

O God, whose fatherly care reaches to the uttermost parts of the earth: We humbly beseech you graciously to behold and bless those whom we love, now absent from us. Defend them from all dangers of soul and body; and grant that both they and we, drawing nearer to you, may be bound together by your love in the communion of your Holy Spirit, and in the fellowship of your saints; through Jesus Christ our Lord. *Amen.*

21. For Those we Love

Almighty God, we entrust all who are dear to us to your never-failing care and love, for this life and the life to come, knowing that you are doing for them better things than we can desire or pray for; through Jesus Christ our Lord. *Amen.*

22. For a Person in Trouble

O merciful God, you have taught us in your holy Word that you desire good things for all your children: Look with pity upon your servant *N.* in *his* time of trouble. Remember *him,* O Lord, in mercy, nourish *his* soul with patience, comfort *him* with a sense of your goodness, let your blessing be upon *him,* and give *him* peace; through Jesus Christ our Lord. *Amen.*

23. For the Victims of Addiction

O blessed Lord, you ministered to all who came to you: Look with compassion upon all who through addiction have lost their health and freedom. Restore to them the assurance of your unfailing mercy; remove from them the fears that beset them; strengthen them in the work of their recovery; and to those who care for them, give patient understanding and persevering love. *Amen.*

24. For the Wounded

Have mercy, O God, on all those who today are wounded and suffering. Since their families and friends are far away, let your grace be their comfort. Raise them to health again, if that is your will for them, but chiefly give them patience and faith in you; through Jesus Christ our Lord. *Amen.*

25. For Sick or Wounded Persons

O Lord, look down from heaven: Behold, visit, and relieve your *servants, NN.* Look upon *them* with the eyes of your mercy, give *them* comfort and sure confidence in you, defend *them* in all danger, and keep *them* in perpetual peace and safety; through Jesus Christ our Lord. *Amen.*

26. A Jewish Prayer on Behalf of the Sick

O Lord God, you are gracious and merciful; you spread your wings of protection and tender care over all your creatures; you heal the sick and bind up their wounds. Receive, we beseech you, our humble petition on behalf of *N.* who is confined to the bed of pain and sickness.

Send *him*, O God, your healing, that *he* may speedily recover from the illness that has come upon *him.* Sustain *his* spirit, relieve *his* pain, and restore *him* to perfect health, happiness, and usefulness. Instill into *his* impaired body the balm of Gilead that *he* may be able to bear testimony to your everlasting mercy and love, for you, O Lord, are a faithful and merciful healer. *Amen.*

27. For Recovery from Sickness

O God, the strength of the weak and the comfort of sufferers: Mercifully accept our prayers, and grant to your servant *N.* the help of your power, that *his* sickness may be turned into health, and our sorrow into joy; through Jesus Christ our Lord. *Amen.*

28. For a Sick Child

Heavenly Father, watch with us over your child *N.*, and grant that *he* may be restored to that perfect health which it is yours alone to give; through Jesus Christ our Lord. *Amen.*

29. A Prayer for Use by a Sick Person

O Father of mercies and God of all comfort: Look upon me and stay with me in this time of weakness and pain. Strengthen my soul and my body, and drive away from me all fear, depression, resentment, and every other bitter mood or evil thought. Bless the doctors, nurses, medics, and all others who are helping me to stay alive and to recover. Help me to cooperate with them patiently and cheerfully. Grant that in time I may be healed, and that I may not forget your goodness to me. Finally, O God, have mercy on those whose suffering is worse than my own. I ask all this through Jesus Christ my Savior. *Amen.*

30. For the Departed

O God, who by the glorious resurrection of your Son Jesus Christ destroyed death, and brought life and immortality to light: Grant that your servant *N.*, being raised with him, may know the strength of his presence, and rejoice in his eternal glory; who with you and the Holy Spirit lives and reigns, one God, for ever and ever. *Amen.*

31. For the Departed

O God, whose mercies cannot be numbered: Accept our prayers on behalf of your servant *N.*, and grant *him* an entrance into the land of light and joy, in the fellowship of your saints; through Jesus Christ our Lord. *Amen.*

32. For the Departed

O God of grace and glory, we remember before you this day our brother (sister) *N.* We thank you for giving *him* to us, *his* [family and] friends, to know and to love as a companion on our earthly pilgrimage. In your boundless compassion, console us who mourn. Give us faith to see in death the gate of eternal life, so that in quiet confidence we may continue our course on earth, until, by your call, we are reunited with those who have gone before; through Jesus Christ our Lord. *Amen.*

33. For Those who have Given their Lives

Almighty God, our heavenly Father, in whose hands are the living and the dead: We give you thanks for all your servants who have laid down their lives in the service of their country. Grant to them your mercy and the light of your presence; and give us such a lively sense of your righteous will, that the work which you have begun in them may be perfected; through Jesus Christ your Son our Lord. *Amen.*

34. For Those who Mourn

Almighty God, Father of mercies and giver of comfort: Deal graciously, we pray, with all who mourn; that, casting all their care on you, they may know the consolation of your love; through Jesus Christ our Lord. *Amen.*

35. For Quiet Confidence

O God of peace, you have taught us that in returning and rest we shall be saved, in quietness and in confidence shall be our strength: By the might of your Spirit lift us, we pray you, to your presence, where we may be still and know that you are God; through Jesus Christ our Lord. *Amen.*

36. A Prayer of Self-Dedication

Almighty and eternal God, so draw our hearts to you, so guide our minds, so fill our imaginations, so control our wills, that we may be wholly yours, utterly dedicated to you; and then use us, we pray you, as you will, and always to your glory and the welfare of your people; through our Lord and Savior Jesus Christ. *Amen.*

37. A Prayer attributed to St. Francis

Lord, make us instruments of your peace. Where there is hatred, let us sow love; where there is injury, pardon; where there is discord, union; where there is doubt, faith; where there is despair, hope; where there is darkness, light; where there is sadness, joy. Grant that we may not so much seek to be consoled as to console; to be understood as to understand; to be loved as to love. For it is in giving that we receive; it is in pardoning that we are pardoned; and it is in dying that we are born to eternal life. *Amen.*

38. Before Receiving Communion

Be present, be present, O Jesus, our great High Priest, as you were present with your disciples, and be known to us in the breaking of bread. *Amen.*

39. After Receiving Communion

God our Father, whose Son our Lord Jesus Christ in a wonderful Sacrament has left us a memorial of his passion: Grant us so to venerate the sacred mysteries of his Body and Blood, that we may ever perceive within ourselves the fruit of his redemption; who lives and reigns with you and the Holy Spirit, one God, for ever and ever. *Amen.*

40. Grace at Meals

Bless, O Lord, your gifts to our use and us to your service; for Christ's sake.

For these and all his mercies, God's holy Name be blessed and praised; through Jesus Christ our Lord. *Amen.*

41. The General Thanksgiving

Almighty God, Father of all mercies, we your unworthy servants give you humble thanks for all your goodness and loving-kindness to us and to all whom you have made. We bless you for our creation, preservation, and all the blessings of this life; but above all for your immeasurable love in the redemption of the world by our Lord Jesus Christ; for the means of grace, and for the hope of glory. And, we pray, give us such an awareness of your mercies, that with truly thankful hearts we may show forth your praise, not only with our lips, but in our lives, by giving up our selves to your service, and by walking before you in holiness and righteousness all our days; through Jesus Christ our Lord, to whom, with you and the Holy Spirit, be honor and glory throughout all ages. *Amen.*

42. A Thanksgiving for the Saints

O God, the King of saints, we praise and glorify your holy Name for all your servants who have finished their course in your faith and fear: for the blessed Virgin Mary; for the holy patriarchs, prophets, apostles, and martyrs; and for all your other righteous servants, known to us and unknown; and we pray that, encouraged by their examples, aided by their prayers, and strengthened by their fellowship, we also may be partakers of the inheritance of the saints in light; through the merits of your Son Jesus Christ our Lord. *Amen.*

43. Blessings

May the God of hope fill us with all joy and peace in believing through the power of the Holy Spirit. *Amen.*

Glory to God whose power, working in us, can do infinitely more than we can ask or imagine: Glory to him from generation to generation in the Church, and in Christ Jesus for ever and ever. *Amen.*

The Lord bless us and keep us. The Lord make his face to shine upon us and be gracious to us. The Lord lift up his countenance upon us and give us peace. *Amen.*

44. Oración de San Francisco de Asís

Señor, haznos instrumentos de tu paz. Donde haya odio, sembremos amor; donde haya ofensa, perdón; donde haya discordia, unión; donde haya duda, fe; donde haya desesperación, esperanza; donde haya tinieblas, luz; donde haya tristeza, gozo. Concede que no busquemos ser consolados, sino consolar; ser comprendidos, sino comprender; ser amados, sino amar. Porque dando, es como recibimos; perdonando, es como somos perdonados; y muriendo, es como nacemos a la vida eterna. *Amén.*

45. Antes de comulgar

¡Hazte presente! Hazte presente, oh Jesús, nuestro gran Sumo Sacerdote, así como te hiciste presente con tus discípulos, y muéstrate a nosotros en la fracción del Pan; tú que vives y reinas con el Padre y el Espíritu Santo, ahora y por siempre. *Amén.*

46. Después de comulgar

Oh Señor Jesucristo, que en un Sacramento maravilloso nos has dejado el memorial de tu pasión: Concédenos, te suplicamos, que de tal modo veneremos los sagrados misterios de tu Cuerpo y Sangre, que discernamos constantemente en nosotros el fruto de tu redención; tú que vives y reinas con el Padre y el Espíritu Santo, un solo Dios, por los siglos de los siglos. *Amén.*

47. Acción de Gracias por los alimentos

Bendice, oh Señor, estos tus dones para nuestro uso, y a nosotros en tu servicio; por amor de Cristo. *Amén.*

48. Acción de Gracias por los Santos

Oh Dios, Rey de los santos, alabamos y glorificamos tu santo Nombre por todos tus siervos que han terminado su carrera en tu fe y temor: por la bendita Virgen María; por los santos patriarcas, profetas, apóstoles y mártires; y por todos tus demás siervos justos, tanto conocidos como desconocides; y te rogamos que nosotros, estimulados por su ejemplo, ayudados por sus oraciones y fortalecidos por su comunión, seamos también partícipes de la herencia de los santos en luz; por los méritos de tu Hijo Jesucristo nuestro Señor. *Amén.*

49. Bendiciones

Gloria a Dios, cuyo poder, actuando en nosotros, puede realizar todas las cosas infinitamente mejor de lo que podemos pedir o pensar: Gloria a El en la Iglesia de generación en generación y en Cristo Jesús por siglos de los siglos. *Amén.*

Que el Dios de la esperanza nos colme de todo gozo y paz en nuestra fe, por el poder del Espíritu Santo. *Amén.*

La gracia de nuestro Señor Jesucristo, el amor de Dios y la comunión del Espíritu Santo sean con todos nosotros, ahora y siempre. *Amén.*

Hymns

HYMNS

Through the centuries, men and women have written hymns in praise and honor of God. Those in this book are only a few of the thousands upon thousands that have been written. Some of those that follow are very old, some are new. Some are translations from Latin, Greek, or German. Some are English, some are Spanish, some are Afro-American spirituals, some are folk hymns.

These hymns have been selected primarily for use in private devotion, rather than in public worship. Since they are intended to be used as prayers, instead of being sung, no music is provided. Music for all the hymns in English can, however, be found in *The Hymnal 1982*, published by the Episcopal Church. Music for many of them can also be found in the *Book of Worship for United States Forces*. Music for the two Spanish hymns can be found in *Albricias*, available from the National Hispanic Office at the Episcopal Church Center.

A GUIDE TO THE HYMNS

FOR THE CHURCH YEAR

Morning 1
Evening 2, 3
Sunday 4
Advent 5, 6, 20
Christmas 7, 8, 9
Epiphany through the following Sunday 10
Lent 11, 28, 29, 30
Holy Week 12, 13
Easter 14, 15, 18, 23
Ascension Day 16, 24
The Day of Pentecost 17, 18
Trinity Sunday 21, 26
Saints' Days 26, 21, 24
Thanksgiving and other National Days 23, 25

FOR PARTICULAR NEEDS

Baptism and Confirmation 17, 18, 23, 28, 29
Christ as Savior and Lord 24, 28, 30
Christian Discipleship and Mission 22, 25, 27, 30
Church and Communion of Saints 21, 24, 25, 26, 27
Holy Communion 19, 20, 24, 28
Holy Spirit 17
Holy Trinity 21, 23
Hymns in Spanish 22, 27
Praise and Gratitude to God 21, 23, 24
Repentance and Forgiveness 29, 30
Spirituals 8, 12, 19, 30

1

Latin, 6th Cent.; st. 1, tr. John Mason Neale (1818-1866);
sts. 2-4, tr. Peter Scagnelli (b. 1949);
st. 5, Charles Coffin (1676-1749); tr. John Chandler (1806-1897)

1 Now that the daylight fills the sky,
  we lift our hearts to God on high,
  that he, in all we do or say,
  would keep us free from harm this day:

2 Our hearts and lips may he restrain;
  keep us from causing others pain,
  that we may see and serve his Son,
  and grow in love for everyone.

3 From evil may he guard our eyes,
  our ears from empty praise and lies;
  from selfishness our hearts release,
  that we may serve, and know his peace;

4 that we, when this new day is gone,
  and night in turn is drawing on,
  with conscience free from sin and blame,
  may praise and bless his holy Name.

5 To God the Father, heavenly Light,
  to Christ, revealed in earthly night,
  to God the Holy Ghost we raise
  our equal and unceasing praise.

2

Mozarabic (Spanish) c. 10th cent.;
tr. Alan G. McDougall (1895-1964);
rev. Anne K. LeCroy (b. 1930)

1 Christ, mighty Savior, Light of all creation,
  you make the daytime radiant with the sunlight
  and to the night give glittering adornment,
        stars in the heavens.

2 Now comes the day's end as the sun is setting:
  mirror of daybreak, pledge of resurrection;
  while in the heavens choirs of stars appearing
        hallow the nightfall.

3 Therefore we come now evening rites to offer,
joyfully chanting holy hymns to praise you,
with all creation joining hearts and voices
    singing your glory.

4 Give heed, we pray you, to our supplication:
that you may grant us pardon for offenses,
strength for our weak hearts, rest for aching bodies,
    soothing the weary.

5 Though bodies slumber, hearts shall keep their vigil,
for ever resting in the peace of Jesus,
in light or darkness worshiping our Savior
    now and for ever.

3

Thomas Ken (1637-1711)

1 All praise to thee, my God, this night,
for all the blessings of the light:
keep me, O keep me, King of kings,
beneath thine own almighty wings.

2 Forgive me, Lord, for thy dear Son,
the ill that I this day have done;
that with the world, myself, and thee,
I, ere I sleep, at peace may be.

3 O may my soul on thee repose,
and with sweet sleep mine eyelids close;
sleep that shall me more vigorous make
to serve my God when I awake.

4 Praise God, from whom all blessings flow;
praise him, all creatures here below;
praise him above, ye heavenly host:
praise Father, Son, and Holy Ghost.

4

Sts. 1 & 2, Christopher Wordsworth (1807-1835), alt.;
st. 3, Charles P. Price (b. 1920);
st. 4, Hymnal 1982

1 O day of radiant gladness,
    O day of joy and light,
O balm of care and sadness,
    most beautiful, most bright;
this day the high and lowly,
    through ages joined in tune,
sing, "Holy, holy, holy,"
    to the great God Triune.

2 This day at the creation,
    the light first had its birth;
this day for our salvation
    Christ rose from depth of earth;
this day our Lord victorious
    the Spirit sent from heaven,
and thus this day most glorious
    a triple light was given.

3 This day, God's people meeting,
    his Holy Scripture hear;
his living presence greeting,
    through Bread and Wine made near.
We journey on, believing,
    renewed with heavenly might,
from grace more grace receiving
    on this blest day of light.

4 That light our hope sustaining,
    we walk the pilgrim way,
at length our rest attaining,
    our endless Sabbath day.
We sing to thee our praises,
    O Father, Spirit, Son;
the Church her voice upraises
    to thee, blest Three in One.

5

Latin, 9th cent.;
ver. Hymnal 1940, alt.

1 Creator of the stars of night,
   your people's everlasting light,
   O Christ, Redeemer of us all,
   we pray you hear us when we call.

2 In sorrow that the ancient curse
   should doom to death a universe,
   you came, O Savior, to set free
   your own in glorious liberty.

3 When this old world drew on toward night,
   you came; but not in splendor bright,
   not as a monarch, but the child
   of Mary, blameless mother mild.

4 At your great Name, O Jesus, now
   all knees must bend, all hearts must bow:
   all things on earth with one accord,
   like those in heaven, shall call you Lord.

5 Come in your holy might, we pray,
   redeem us for eternal day;
   defend us while we dwell below
   from all assaults of our dread foe.

6 To God the Father, God the Son,
   and God the Spirit, Three in One,
   praise, honor, might, and glory be
   from age to age eternally.

6

Charles Wesley (1707-1788)

1 Come, thou long-expected Jesus,
      born to set thy people free;
   from our fears and sins release us,
      let us find our rest in thee.

2 Israel's strength and consolation,
    hope of all the earth thou art:
dear desire of every nation,
    joy of every longing heart.

3 Born thy people to deliver,
    born a child, and yet a king,
born to reign in us for ever,
    now thy gracious kingdom bring.

4 By thine own eternal Spirit
    rule in all our hearts alone;
by thine all-sufficient merit
    raise us to thy glorious throne.

7

John Francis Wade (1711-1786);
tr. Frederick Oakeley (1802-1880) and others

1   O come, all ye faithful,
      joyful and triumphant,
O come ye, O come ye to Bethlehem;
    come, and behold him,
      born the King of angels;

Refrain   O come, let us adore him,
           O come, let us adore him,
           O come, let us adore him,
           Christ the Lord.

2   God from God,
      Light from Light eternal,
lo! he abhors not the Virgin's womb;
    only-begotten
      Son of the Father;

        Refrain

3 Sing, choirs of angels,
    sing in exultation,
sing, all ye citizens of heaven above;
    glory to God,
    glory in the highest;

    Refrain

4 Yea, Lord, we greet thee,
    born this happy morning;
Jesus, to thee be glory given;
    Word of the Father,
    now in flesh appearing;

    Refrain

8
                                    Afro-American spiritual, 19th cent.;
                                    adapt. John W. Work (b. 1901)

Refrain Go tell it on the mountain,
        over the hills and everywhere;
      go tell it on the mountain,
        that Jesus Christ is born!

1 While shepherds kept their watching
    o'er silent flocks by night,
behold, throughout the heavens
    there shone a holy light.

    Refrain

2 The shepherds feared and trembled
    when lo! above the earth
rang out the angel chorus
    that hailed our Savior's birth.

    Refrain

3 Down in a lowly manger
    the humble Christ was born,
and God sent us salvation
    that blessed Christmas morn.

    Refrain

9

Joseph Mohr (1792-1848);
tr. John Freeman Young (1820-1885)

1 Silent night, holy night,
all is calm, all is bright
round yon virgin mother and child.
Holy infant, so tender and mild,
sleep in heavenly peace.
Sleep in heavenly peace.

2 Silent night, holy night,
shepherds quake at the sight,
glories stream from heaven afar,
heavenly hosts sing alleluia;
Christ, the Savior, is born!
Christ, the Savior, is born!

3 Silent night, holy night,
Son of God, love's pure light
radiant beams from thy holy face,
with the dawn of redeeming grace,
Jesus, Lord, at thy birth.
Jesus, Lord, at thy birth.

10

Caelius Sedulius (5th cent.);
st. 1, tr. The Hymn Book of the Anglican Church of Canada
and the United Church of Canada, 1971;
sts. 2-5, tr. John Mason Neale (1818-1866), alt.

1 When Christ's appearing was made known,
King Herod trembled for his throne;
but he who offers heavenly birth
sought not the kingdoms of this earth.

2 The eastern sages saw from far
and followed on his guiding star;
by light their way to Light they trod,
and by their gifts confessed their God.

3 Within the Jordan's sacred flood
  the heavenly Lamb in meekness stood,
  that he, to whom no sin was known,
  might cleanse his people from their own.

4 Oh, what a miracle divine,
  when water reddened into wine!
  He spoke the word, and forth it flowed
  in streams that nature ne'er bestowed.

5 All glory, Jesus, be to thee
  for this thy glad epiphany:
  whom with the Father we adore
  and Holy Ghost for evermore.

11

Latin, 6th cent.;
tr. Maurice F. Bell (1862-1947), alt.

1 The glory of these forty days
  we celebrate with songs of praise;
  for Christ, through whom all things were made,
  himself has fasted and has prayed.

2 Alone and fasting Moses saw
  the loving God who gave the law;
  and to Elijah, fasting, came
  the steeds and chariots of flame.

3 So Daniel trained his mystic sight,
  delivered from the lions' might;
  and John, the Bridegroom's friend, became
  the herald of Messiah's name.

4 Then grant us, Lord, like them to be
  full oft in fast and prayer with thee;
  our spirits strengthened with thy grace,
  and give us joy to see thy face.

12 *Afro-American spiritual*

1 Were you there when they crucified my Lord?
  Were you there when they crucified my Lord?
  Oh! Sometimes it causes me to tremble, tremble, tremble.
  Were you there when they crucified my Lord?

2 Were you there when they nailed him to the tree?
  Were you there when they nailed him to the tree?
  Oh! Sometimes it causes me to tremble, tremble, tremble.
  Were you there when they nailed him to the tree?

3 Were you there when they pierced him in the side?
  Were you there when they pierced him in the side?
  Oh! Sometimes it causes me to tremble, tremble, tremble.
  Were you there when they pierced him in the side?

4 Were you there when they laid him in the tomb?
  Were you there when they laid him in the tomb?
  Oh! Sometimes it causes me to tremble, tremble, tremble.
  Were you there when they laid him in the tomb?

13 *Venantius Honorius Fortunatus (540?-600?);*
ver. Hymnal 1982, after John Mason Neale (1818-1866)

1 Sing, my tongue, the glorious battle;
    of the mighty conflict sing;
  tell the triumph of the victim,
    to his cross thy tribute bring.
  Jesus Christ, the world's Redeemer
    from that cross now reigns as King.

2 Thirty years among us dwelling,
    his appointed time fulfilled,
  born for this, he meets his passion,
    this the Savior freely willed:
  on the cross the Lamb is lifted,
    where his precious blood is spilled.

3 He endures the nails, the spitting,
  vinegar, and spear, and reed;
from that holy body broken
  blood and water forth proceed:
earth, and stars, and sky, and ocean,
  by that flood from stain are freed.

4 Faithful cross! above all other,
  one and only noble tree!
None in foliage, none in blossom,
  none in fruit thy peer may be:
sweetest wood and sweetest iron!
  sweetest weight is hung on thee.

5 Bend thy boughs, O tree of glory!
  Thy relaxing sinews bend;
for awhile the ancient rigor
  that thy birth bestowed, suspend;
and the King of heavenly beauty
  gently on thine arms extend.

14

Latin, 14th cent.; tr. Lyra Davidica, 1708, alt.
st. 4, Charles Wesley (1707-1788)

1 Jesus Christ is risen today, Alleluia!
  our triumphant holy day, Alleluia!
  who did once upon the cross, Alleluia!
  suffer to redeem our loss. Alleluia!

2 Hymns of praise then let us sing, Alleluia!
  unto Christ, our heavenly King, Alleluia!
  who endured the cross and grave, Alleluia!
  sinners to redeem and save. Alleluia!

3 But the pains which he endured, Alleluia!
  our salvation have procured, Alleluia!
  now above the sky he's King, Alleluia!
  where the angels ever sing. Alleluia!

4 Sing we to our God above, Alleluia!
  praise eternal as his love, Alleluia!
  praise him, all ye heavenly host, Alleluia!
  Father, Son, and Holy Ghost. Alleluia!

15

Latin, 1632;
tr. Robert Campbell (1814-1868), alt.

1 At the Lamb's high feast we sing
   praise to our victorious King,
   who hath washed us in the tide
   flowing from his piercèd side;
   praise we him, whose love divine
   gives his sacred Blood for wine,
   gives his Body for the feast,
   Christ the victim, Christ the priest.

2 Where the Paschal blood is poured,
   death's dark angel sheathes his sword;
   Israel's hosts triumphant go
   through the wave that drowns the foe.
   Praise we Christ, whose blood was shed,
   Paschal victim, Paschal bread;
   with sincerity and love
   eat we manna from above.

3 Mighty victim from on high,
   hell's fierce powers beneath thee lie;
   thou hast conquered in the fight,
   thou hast brought us life and light:
   now no more can death appall,
   now no more the grave enthrall;
   thou hast opened paradise,
   and in thee thy saints shall rise.

4 Easter triumph, Easter joy,
   these alone do sin destroy.
   From sin's power do thou set free
   souls new-born, O Lord, in thee.
   Hymns of glory, songs of praise,
   Father, unto thee we raise:
   risen Lord, all praise to thee
   with the Spirit ever be.

16

The Venerable Bede (673-735);
sts. 1 & 2, tr. Elizabeth Rundle Charles (1828-1896), alt.;
st. 3, tr. Benjamin Webb (1819-1885), alt.

1 A hymn of glory let us sing,
   new hymns throughout the world shall ring;
   by a new way none ever trod
   Christ takes his place—the throne of God!

2 You are a present joy, O Lord;
   you will be ever our reward;
   and great the light in you we see
   to guide us to eternity.

3 O risen Christ, ascended Lord,
   all praise to you let earth accord,
   who are, while endless ages run,
   with Father and with Spirit, One.

17

Latin, 12th cent.;
tr. Charles P. Price (b. 1920)

1 Come, thou Holy Spirit bright;
   come with thy celestial light;
     pour on us thy love divine.
   Come, protector of the poor;
   come, thou source of blessing sure;
     come within our hearts to shine.

2 Thou, of comforters the best,
   thou, the soul's most welcome guest,
     of our peace thou art the sign.
   In our labor, be our aid;
   in our summer, cooling shade.
     Every bitter tear refine.

3 Brighter than the noonday sun,
   fill our lives which Christ has won;
     fill our hearts and make them thine.
   Where thou art not, we have nought:
   all our word and deed and thought
     twisted from thy true design.

4 Bend the stubborn heart and will;
  melt the frozen, warm the chill;
    rule us by thy judgment's line.
  Cleanse us with thy healing power;
  what is barren bring to flower;
    to thy love our sins consign.

5 To thy people who adore
  and confess thee evermore,
    thy blest sevenfold gift assign.
  Grant us thy salvation, Lord,
  boundless mercy our reward,
    joys which earth and heaven entwine.

18   *John Brownlow Geyer (b. 1932). alt.*

1 We know that Christ is raised and dies no more.
  Embraced by death he broke its fearful hold;
  and our despair he turned to blazing joy.
    Alleluia!

2 We share by water in his saving death,
  Reborn we share with him an Easter life
  as living members of a living Christ.
    Alleluia!

3 The Father's splendor clothes the Son with life.
  The Spirit's power shakes the Church of God.
  Baptized we live with God the Three in One.
    Alleluia!

4 A new creation comes to life and grows
  as Christ's new body takes on flesh and blood.
  The universe restored and whole will sing:
    Alleluia!

19

Afro-American spiritual

1 Let us break bread together on our knees;
let us break bread together on our knees;

Refrain: when I fall on my knees,
with my face to the rising sun,
O Lord, have mercy on me.

2 Let us drink wine together on our knees;
let us drink wine together on our knees;

Refrain

3 Let us praise God together on our knees;
let us praise God together on our knees;
Refrain

20

*Liturgy of St. James;
para. Gerard Moultrie (1829-1885)*

1 Let all mortal flesh keep silence,
and with fear and trembling stand;
ponder nothing earthly-minded,
for with blessing in his hand
Christ our God to earth descendeth,
our full homage to demand.

2 King of kings, yet born of Mary,
as of old on earth he stood,
Lord of lords in human vesture,
in the Body and the Blood
he will give to all the faithful
his own self for heavenly food.

3 Rank on rank the host of heaven
spreads its vanguard on the way,
as the Light of Light descendeth
from the realms of endless day,
that the powers of hell may vanish
as the darkness clears away.

4 At his feet the six-winged seraph;
   cherubim with sleepless eye,
veil their faces to the Presence,
   as with ceaseless voice they cry,
"Alleluia, alleluia!
   Alleluia, Lord Most High!"

21

Reginald Heber (1783-1826), alt.

1 Holy, holy, holy! Lord God Almighty!
   Early in the morning our song shall rise to thee:
Holy, holy, holy! Merciful and mighty,
   God in three Persons, blessèd Trinity.

2 Holy, holy, holy! All the saints adore thee,
   casting down their golden crowns around the glassy sea;
cherubim and seraphim falling down before thee,
   which wert, and art, and evermore shalt be.

3 Holy, holy, holy! Though the darkness hide thee,
   though the sinful human eye thy glory may not see,
only thou art holy; there is none beside thee,
   perfect in power, in love, and purity.

4 Holy, holy, holy! Lord God Almighty!
   All thy works shall praise thy Name,
   in earth, and sky, and sea;
Holy, holy, holy! Merciful and mighty,
   God in three Persons, blessèd Trinity.

22

Cesareo Gabarain

1 Tú has venido a la orilla,
   no has buscado ni a sabios ni a ricos,
   tan sólo quieres que yo te siga.

   Estribillo: Señor, me has mirado a los ojos
               y sonriendo has dicho mi nombre;
               en la arena he dejado mi barca;
               junto a ti buscaré otro mar.

² Tú sabes bien lo que tengo:
   En mi barca no hay oro ni espadas,
tan sólo redes y mi trabajo.

Estribillo

³ Tú necesitas mis manos,
   mi cansancio que a otros descanse,
amor que quiera seguir amando.

Estribillo

⁴ Tú, pescador de otros mares,
   ansia eterna de almas que esperan,
amigo bueno, que así me llamas.

Estribillo

23

Martin Rinckart (1586-1649);
tr. Catherine Winkworth (1827-1878), alt.

¹ Now thank we all our God,
   with heart, and hands, and voices,
who wondrous things hath done,
   in whom his world rejoices;
who from our mother's arms
   hath blessed us on our way
with countless gifts of love,
   and still is ours today.

² O may this bounteous God
   through all our life be near us!
with ever-joyful hearts
   and blessed peace to cheer us;
and keep us in his grace,
   and guide us when perplexed,
and free us from all ills
   in this world and the next.

3 All praise and thanks to God
   the Father now be given,
the Son, and him who reigns
   with them in highest heaven,
eternal, Triune God,
   whom earth and heaven adore;
for thus it was, is now,
   and shall be, evermore.

24   *William Chatterton Dix (1837-1898)*

1 Alleluia! sing to Jesus!
   his the scepter, his the throne;
Alleluia! his the triumph,
   his the victory alone;
Hark! the songs of peaceful Zion
   thunder like a mighty flood;
Jesus out of every nation
   hath redeemed us by his blood.

2 Alleluia! not as orphans
   are we left in sorrow now;
Alleluia! he is near us,
   faith believes, nor questions how:
though the cloud from sight received him,
   when the forty days were o'er,
shall our hearts forget his promise,
   "I am with you evermore?"

3 Alleluia! Bread of Heaven,
   thou on earth our food, our stay!
Alleluia! here the sinful
   flee to thee from day to day:
Intercessor, friend of sinners,
   earth's Redeemer, plead for me,
where the songs of all the sinless
   sweep across the crystal sea.

⁴ Alleluia! King eternal,
    thee the Lord of lords we own:
Alleluia! born of Mary,
    earth thy footstool, heaven thy throne:
thou within the veil hast entered,
    robed in flesh, our great High Priest:
thou on earth both Priest and Victim
    in the eucharistic feast.

25 *John Oxenham (1852-1941), alt.*

¹ In Christ there is no East or West,
    in him no South or North,
but one great fellowship of love
    throughout the whole wide earth.

² Join hands, disciples of the faith,
    whate'er your race may be!
Who serves my Father as his child
    is surely kin to me.

³ In Christ now meet both East and West,
    in Him meet South and North,
all Christly souls are one in him,
    throughout the whole wide earth.

26 *John Athelstan Laurie Riley (1858-1945)*

¹ Ye watchers and ye holy ones,
    bright seraphs, cherubim, and thrones,
      raise the glad strain, Alleluia!
Cry out, dominions, princedoms, powers,
virtues, archangels, angels' choirs,
      Alleluia, alleluia, alleluia, alleluia, alleluia!

2 O higher than the cherubim,
   more glorious than the seraphim,
      lead their praises, Alleluia!
   Thou bearer of the eternal Word,
   most gracious, magnify the Lord,
      Alleluia, alleluia, alleluia, alleluia, alleluia!

3 Respond, ye souls in endless rest,
   ye patriarchs and prophets blest,
      Alleluia, alleluia!
   Ye holy twelve, ye martyrs strong,
   all saints triumphant, raise the song,
      Alleluia, alleluia, alleluia, alleluia, alleluia!

4 O friends, in gladness let us sing,
   supernal anthems echoing,
      Alleluia, alleluia!
   To God the Father, God the Son,
   and God the Spirit, Three in One,
      Alleluia, alleluia, alleluia, alleluia, alleluia!

27   *Cesareo Gabarain*

Estribillo: Juntos como hermanos, miembros de una Iglesia,
              vamos caminando al encuentro del Señor.

1 Un largo caminar por el desierto bajo el sol;
   no podemos avanzar sin la ayuda del Señor.

            Estribillo

2 Unidos al rezar, unidos en una canción,
   viviremos nuestra fe con la ayuda del Señor.

            Estribillo

3 La Iglesia en marcha está; a un mundo nuevo vamos ya
   donde reinará el amor, donde reinará la paz.

            Estribillo

28

Henry Williams Baker (1821-1877);
para. of Psalm 23

1 The King of love my shepherd is,
    whose goodness faileth never;
I nothing lack if I am his,
    and he is mine for ever.

2 Where streams of living water flow,
    my ransomed soul he leadeth,
and where the verdant pastures grow,
    with food celestial feedeth.

3 Perverse and foolish oft I strayed,
    but yet in love he sought me,
and on his shoulder gently laid,
    and home, rejoicing, brought me.

4 In death's dark vale I fear no ill
    with thee, dear Lord, beside me;
thy rod and staff my comfort still,
    thy cross before to guide me.

5 Thou spread'st a table in my sight;
    thy unction grace bestoweth;
and oh, what transport of delight
    from thy pure chalice floweth!

6 And so through all the length of days
    thy goodness faileth never:
Good Sheperd, may I sing thy praise
    within thy house for ever.

29

John Newton (1725-1807), alt.;
st. 5, John Rees (19th cent.)

1 Amazing grace! how sweet the sound,
    that saved a wretch like me!
I once was lost but now am found,
    was blind but now I see.

2 'Twas grace that taught my heart to fear,
　　and grace my fears relieved;
　how precious did that grace appear
　　the hour I first believed!

3 The Lord has promised good to me,
　　his word my hope secures;
　he will my shield and portion be
　　as long as life endures.

4 Through many dangers, toils, and snares,
　　I have already come;
　'tis grace that brought me safe thus far,
　　and grace will lead me home.

5 When we've been there ten thousand years,
　　bright shining as the sun,
　we've no less days to sing God's praise
　　than when we'd first begun.

30 *Afro-American spiritual*

Refrain: There is a balm in Gilead,
　　　　　　　to make the wounded whole,
　　　　　　there is a balm in Gilead,
　　　　　　　to heal the sin-sick soul.

1 Sometimes I feel discouraged,
　　and think my work's in vain,
　but then the Holy Spirit
　　revives my soul again.

　　　　　Refrain

2 If you cannot preach like Peter,
　　if you cannot pray like Paul,
　you can tell the love of Jesus,
　　and say, "He died for all."

　　　　　Refrain

THE CHURCH YEAR

SEASONS OF THE YEAR

The Church Year begins with the Season of Advent, which starts on the Sunday that falls on or closest to November 30. Christmas comes in the week following the Fourth Sunday of Advent. Advent is a Latin word meaning "coming," and during it we look forward to Jesus' coming in glory at the end of time and to the coming celebration of his birth.

Christmas Season lasts twelve days, from Christmas Day (December 25) until the Epiphany (January 6). It includes one or two Sundays.

Epiphany Season extends from January 6 until Ash Wednesday, and includes from four to nine Sundays. The First Sunday after the Epiphany is also the feast of the Baptism of Christ. Epiphany is a Greek word meaning "showing," and in this season we remember many of the ways in which Jesus showed himself to be the Messiah and Son of God.

The Season of Lent lasts from Ash Wednesday until Easter Day. It includes six Sundays and forty weekdays. Lent is the time in which we examine our lives and prepare to renew our baptismal vows at Easter. (See the Baptismal Covenant on page 28).

(For the dates of Ash Wednesday and Easter, see page 156.)

Holy Week is the last week of Lent. It begins on the Sunday of the Passion (Palm Sunday) and includes Maundy Thursday, Good Friday, and Holy Saturday.

Easter Season lasts fifty days, from Easter Day — which is the holiest day in the Church Year — through the Day of Pentecost (which means "fiftieth"). It includes seven "Sundays of Easter" and the feast of the Ascension on the fortieth day (always a Thursday). During this season we rejoice, not only because Jesus rose from the dead, but because in Baptism he has made us sharers in his resurrection and given us his Holy Spirit.

The Season after Pentecost continues until the next Advent, and includes more than twenty Sundays. The First Sunday after Pentecost is also called Trinity Sunday.

OTHER HOLY DAYS

In addition to the Sundays and holy days mentioned above, the Church Year includes what are called "fixed" holy days. Some of these commemorate events in our Lord's life; others are saints' days. All of them, however, have fixed calendar dates and therefore fall on different days of the week in different years. Because of this, their observance can conflict with the celebration of Sunday or some other more important day. When this happens, the normal procedure is to transfer the fixed feast to the next convenient weekday. The exceptions to the rule are the feasts marked with an asterisk (*); when these fall on Sunday, their observance takes the place of the Sunday service.

The major fixed feasts observed during the year are the following. (The New Testament passages listed with each feast usually tell something about the person or event being commemorated.)

†*January 1	The Holy Name of Our Lord Jesus Christ (Luke 2:15-21)
*January 6	The Epiphany of Our Lord Jesus Christ (Matthew 2:1-12)
January 18	The Confession of St. Peter the Apostle (Matthew 16:13-19)
January 25	The Conversion of St. Paul the Apostle (Acts 9:1-31)
†*February 2	The Presentation of Our Lord Jesus Christ in the Temple (Luke 2:22-40)
February 24	Saint Matthias the Apostle (Acts 1:15-26)
March 19	Saint Joseph (Matthew 1:18-25. Luke 2:41-52)
† March 25	The Annunciation of Our Lord Jesus Christ to the Blessed Virgin Mary (Luke 1:26-38)
April 25	Saint Mark the Evangelist (Acts 12:1-25)
May 1	Saint Philip and Saint James [Son of Alphaeus], Apostles (John 14:6-14. Acts 1:12-14)
† May 31	The Visitation of the Blessed Virgin Mary (Luke 1:39-45)
June 11	Saint Barnabas the Apostle (Acts 4:32-37. Acts 11:19-30)
June 24	The Nativity of St. John the Baptist (Luke 1:5-25, 57-66)
June 29	Saint Peter and Saint Paul, Apostles (John 21:15-19, 2 Timothy 4:1-8.)
July 22	Saint Mary Magdalene (John 20:1-18)
July 25	Saint James the Apostle [Son of Zebedee] (Mark 1:14-20. Acts 11:27–12:3)
†*August 6	The Transfiguration of Our Lord Jesus Christ (Luke 9:28-36)

August 15	Saint Mary the Virgin (Luke 1:46-55)
August 24	Saint Bartholomew the Apostle (Mark 3:13-19)
† September 14	Holy Cross Day (Philippians 2:5-11)
September 21	Saint Matthew, Apostle and Evangelist (Matthew 9:9-13)
September 29	Saint Michael and All Angels (Revelation 12:7-12)
October 18	Saint Luke the Evangelist (Philemon 21-25. 2 Timothy 4:5-13)
October 23	Saint James of Jerusalem (Acts 15:1-20)
October 28	Saint Simon and Saint Jude, Apostles (Luke 6:12-16)
*November 1	All Saints (Revelation 7:9-17)
November 30	Saint Andrew the Apostle (John 1:35-42)
December 21	Saint Thomas the Apostle (John 20:24-29)
*December 25	The Nativity of Our Lord Jesus Christ (Luke 2:1-20)
December 26	Saint Stephen, Deacon and Martyr (Acts 6:8—7:60)
December 27	Saint John, Apostle and Evangelist (John 21:20-24)
December 28	The Holy Innocents (Matthew 2:13-18)

The Book of Common Prayer also lists a number of "lesser feasts," the observance of which is optional. Some of these persons are mentioned in Scripture; others are heroes of the faith who lived in later times. In the partial list that follows, the year and place (when not obvious) of death is given in parentheses.

January 21	Agnes, Martyr at Rome (304)
February 4	Cornelius the Centurion (see Acts 10:1-48)
February 13	Absalom Jones, Priest (Philadelphia, 1818)
March 17	Patrick of Ireland, Bishop (461)
March 27	Charles Henry Brent, Bishop (Switzerland, 1929)
April 29	Catherine of Siena, Nun (Italy, 1380)
May 25	The Venerable Bede, Priest and Monk (England, 735)
June 3	The Martyrs of Uganda (East Africa, 1886)
July 29	Mary and Martha of Bethany (see Luke 10:38-42 and John 11:1-44)
August 28	Augustine of Hippo, Bishop (North Africa, 430)
September 28	David Pendleton Oakerhater, Deacon (Oklahoma, 1931)
October 4	Francis of Assisi, Friar (Italy, 1226)
November 11	Martin of Tours, Bishop (France, 397)
November 16	Margaret, Queen of Scotland (1093)
November 28	Kamehameha and Emma, King and Queen of Hawaii (1863, 1885)
December 6	Nicholas of Myra, Bishop (Asia Minor, about 342)

†See the readings and collect for Feasts of Our Lord on page 15.
*Indicates feasts observed on Sunday when they fall on that day.

DATES OF ASH WEDNESDAY AND EASTER

Year	Ash Wednesday	Easter
1988	February 17	April 3
1989	February 8	March 26
1990	February 28	April 15
1991	February 13	March 31
1992	March 4	April 19
1993	February 24	April 11
1994	February 16	April 3
1995	March 1	April 16
1996	February 21	April 7
1997	February 12	March 30
1998	February 25	April 12
1999	February 17	April 4
2000	March 8	April 23
2001	February 28	April 15
2002	February 13	March 31
2003	March 5	April 20
2004	February 25	April 11
2005	February 9	March 27
2006	March 1	April 16
2007	February 21	April 8
2008	February 6	March 23
2009	February 25	April 12
2010	February 5	April 4

ABOUT THE EPISCOPAL CHURCH

The Episcopal Church is one of the twenty-seven national and regional churches of the world-wide Anglican Communion. Most of these churches trace their beginnings to the work of missionaries sent by the Church of England. All together, there are about sixty-one million Anglicans.

Each of these national or regional churches is independent, but they work closely together, and all look for spiritual leadership to the Archbishop of Canterbury. The Church of England itself traces its history back to missionaries who arrived in the British Isles from Gaul (France), Egypt, and Italy in the third through the sixth centuries.

The Episcopal Church in the United States became independent of the Church of England in 1786, shortly after the American Revolution. Perhaps not surprisingly, its method of government (polity) is similar to that of the Federal Government. The church's General Convention, which meets every three years, consists of two houses: the House of Bishops and the House of Deputies (which consists of elected members of the clergy and laity). All changes in church law and policy must be agreed to by both houses.

The faith of the Episcopal Church is the traditional Christian faith handed down from the time of the New Testament. While some churches require their members to accept beliefs that are not mentioned in the Bible, or to interpret the Bible in a particular way, the Anglican churches believe that the Bible itself contains all teaching necessary to salvation.

The Episcopal Church confesses this biblical faith in its worship, proclaiming Jesus Christ to be true God and true Man, who—by his birth, ministry, death, resurrection, and ascension—brought salvation to the world. We also acknowledge that God is Trinity: Father, Son, and Holy Spirit. These basic beliefs are summarized in the two creeds used in our worship, the Apostles' Creed (see the inside covers of this book) and the Nicene Creed (see page 39).

The Episcopal Church also accepts the traditional view that the sacraments are saving events. We believe, for example, that in Holy Baptism we are truly born again in Christ, and that in the Eucharist (Holy Communion) Christ is truly present under the forms of bread and wine. We also believe that he is present in the preaching of his word, and wherever two or three are gathered together in his name (Matthew 18:20).

The chief ministers of the church are the bishops, whose task it is to unify the church and to guard the faith which has been handed down to it. Each bishop has been ordained and consecrated by other bishops, in a line that traces back to the time of the apostles. This continuity of the faith, guarded by the bishops, is called "apostolic succession," and it signifies the continuity of the church today with the church of New Testament times. The other two orders of ordained ministers are the priests (also called presbyters) and the deacons.

Lay people have a place of major importance in the Episcopal Church, both in its government and in its worship. At church services lay people regularly assist in various ways. Some lay ministries require a license from the bishop; others do not.

The Bishop for the Armed Forces regularly licenses lay men and women as "lay readers." These persons assist the chaplain in appropriate ways, and, in the chaplain's absence, lead services of worship. Such licensing is done with the approval of the Senior Chaplain, and after extensive study and training.

INDEX OF BIBLE PASSAGES

GENERAL INDEX

EL PADRE NUESTRO

Padre nuestro que estás en el cielo,
    santificado sea tu Nombre,
    venga tu reino,
    hágase tu voluntad,
        en la tierra como en el cielo.
Danos hoy nuestro pan de cada día.
Perdona nuestras ofensas,
    como también nosotros perdonamos
        a los que nos ofenden.
No nos dejes caer en tentación
    y líbranos del mal.
Porque tuyo es el reino,
    tuyo es el poder,
    y tuya es la gloria,
    ahora y por siempre. Amén.

CREDO DE LOS APÓSTOLES

Creo en Dios Padre todopoderoso,
    creador del cielo y de la tierra.
Creo en Jesucristo, su único Hijo, nuestro Señor.
    Fue concebido por obra y gracia del Espíritu Santo
        y nació de la Virgen María.
    Padeció bajo el poder de Poncio Pilato.
    Fue crucificado, muerto y sepultado.
    Descendió a los infiernos.
    Al tercer día resucitó de entre los muertos.
    Subió a los cielos,
        y está sentado a la diestra de Dios Padre.
    Desde allí ha de venir a juzgar a vivos y muertos.
Creo en el Espíritu Santo,
    la santa Iglesia católica,
    la comunión de los santos,
    el perdón de los pecados,
    la resurrección de los muertos,
    y la vida eterna. Amén.